LIFE IS GREAT!

LIFE IS GREAT!

Revealing the 7 Secrets
to a More Joyful You!

Rabbi Yitz Wyne

Library of Congress Control Number:		2011904757
ISBN:	Hardcover	978-1-4568-6944-1
	Softcover	978-1-4568-6943-4

This book was printed in the United States of America.

To order additional copies of this book, contact:
Xlibris Corporation
1-888-795-4274
www.Xlibris.com
Orders@Xlibris.com
62944

Contents

Enjoy learning and living these 7 secrets for the happy and the soon-to-be happier.

Dedicated to and in honor of

Wifie
My eternal life partner

In the words of Rabbi Akiva when he addressed his students: "All of the Torah wisdom that is mine, all of the Torah wisdom that is yours, all belongs to her (his wife)."

Every meaningful accomplishment that I have been blessed with in the past twenty years has only been granted to me because of you. Thank you for being the best wife to me and mother to our children that anyone could ever imagine.

Our six incredible children
***Chemie, Tali, Shuey, Aharon, Heshy,** and **Rivky**.*
May the Almighty continue to bless you and may you merit to have children who give you as much pleasure and wisdom as you have given Mommy and me.

All seven of you inspire and motivate me every day
to know and to teach others that
Life is Great!

Dedicated to the memory of

My rabbi, teacher, and mentor, the Rosh HaYeshiva of Aish HaTorah in Jerusalem,

Rabbi Noah Weinberg, of blessed memory.

Rabbi Weinberg was literally my spiritual father. Over the twenty-four years that I was privileged to know him; it was he who taught me the majority of my Torah knowledge and Jewish wisdom. Perhaps even more importantly, Rabbi Weinberg taught me how to approach life. His influence can be seen in the best aspects of my personal and professional lives. The majority of concepts that are mentioned in this book I learned directly from Rabbi Weinberg.

Acknowledgments

The only people with whom you should try to get even
are those who have helped you.

—*John E. Southard*

WHEN IT COMES to recognizing the people who have helped me in this project, the question is *not* who to thank, the question is who not to thank!

Several other incredible scholars have had a profound influence in my life for which I am eternally grateful. Most notably Rabbi Yaakov Weinberg of blessed memory, Rabbi Yitzchak Berkowitz, Rabbi Noah Orlowick, Rabbi Gill Eisenbach, Rabbi Zelig Pliskin, and Rabbi Yehonason Berger.

My family plays a vital role in my life. I am particularly grateful to my parents—Blumie Trute, Mel Wyne and Phyllis Nurgitz—and my exceptionally supportive in-laws who are involved in my life on a day-to-day basis, Adrienne and Ray Zetoony.

I have deep gratitude to Rabbi Nate Segal, Rabbi Aryeh Pamensky, Rabbi Aryeh Markman and Rabbi Yehoshua Sauer for their valuable guidance and friendship over the years.

My executive director Amy Henry and my visual arts maven Anne Lubin—thank you both for spending almost every waking hour supporting my mission and doing your best to always make me look good in the eyes of others. Your dedication and loyalty are unwavering and inspire me. Each of your creative talents is evident in all my work, and your consistent input to this and every project is of immeasurable value. Amy, I appreciate your careful rereading of the manuscript for this book and your suggestions on how to improve it as well as our continuous suggestions on how to be better in all we do. Anne, thank you for making everything I produce look so wonderful.

I am especially grateful to my friend, student, and cohost of *The Rabbi Show* radio program, Peter Dubowsky, for being a critical sounding board for every idea in this book.

Thank you to Dr. Richard Rothman for believing in my efforts, and supporting the writing of this book!

Acknowledgements

continued

I HAVE GREAT pleasure in acknowledging the founders, leaders, and congregants of my beloved Young Israel Aish of Las Vegas (YI AISH LV) synagogue community.

Their commitment to our mission and to me as their rabbi inspires me every day. Their unwavering support and loyalty have enabled me to grow as a rabbi, expand my horizons, and bring positive Jewish values to so many.

There are a handful of very special people whom I refer to as my "angels", they have given generously of their hearts and souls, time and resources. If not for their financial and emotional support, I would not be able to do the work that I do. They are all truly heaven-sent and may the Almighty continue to bless their every endeavor!

(Names are listed in alphabetical order)

My heartfelt thanks goes to Simon S. and Mazal Abraham, Steve and Heather Baker, Gary and Tracy Banner, Stan Barbanell, Congresswoman Shelley Berkley and Dr. Larry Lerhner, Dr. David and Lisa Blank, Dr.

Phil and Michelle Devore, Bob and Shelley Dubin, Peter and Donna Dubowsky, Abbie Fink, Yaakov Fuller, David and Yael Ghermezian, Eskander and Debbie Ghermezian, Etan and Renee Goldman, Jeri and Herb* Goldman, Mirium Halabe, Michael and Brandie Huskey, Andy Katz, Les Lazarick, Jay and Hadassa Lefkowitz, Tom and Marla Letizia, Howard and Susan Levy, James Levy, Lisa Mallinger, Dr. Adam and Dee Milman, Alan and Christy Molasky, Michele Mosey, Bruce and Amy Mufson, Mike and Emily Novick, Dr. Mark Ohriner, Evelyn and Ernie Ostreicher, Stephen and Anna Paige, Bob and Kelly Papock, Manny and Rachel Reiser, Paul and Felice Rockoff, Levi and Esther Rothman, Michael and Judy Sapir, Milton I. Schwartz*, Lenard and Geri Schwartzer, Darcy and Elysia Silver, Dr. Aaron and Beth Sroka, Alan and Rhoda Stock, Brian and Jessica Stockman, Andreah Werner, Nathan White, Adrienne and Ray Zetooney.

My deepest gratitude goes to the Almighty,
who has blessed every moment of my existence.
Thank you, G-d for loving me so much.
I ask for Your help to continue sanctifying Your holy name.
May I be worthy of Your patience, compassion, and love
as I strive, along with many others,
to share and increase those same qualities
among my fellow human beings.

**deceased*

Author's Notes

LIFE IS GREAT is essentially a compilation of the past twenty-seven years of Torah study as well as my twenty years experience as a rabbi, husband, and father. My primary motivation in embarking in this project was to put into writing and elucidate the most important concepts that I wish to pass on to my children.

There are many people, books, and articles that I have used to compile the wisdom and concepts in this book. The depth of gratitude that I feel toward all who have contributed to this work cannot be expressed in words, for it is too great.

Whereas it is a Talmudic principle to "say wisdom in the name of the one who said it," if it will be less cumbersome for the reader to absorb the information, Jewish law permits one to teach concepts without giving credit where credit is due. Because of the nature of this work, I have chosen not to cite specific sources for the many pieces of wisdom contained herein.

I learned this valuable lesson many years ago while speaking with my sister Shari. In the middle of the conversation, after I had mentioned several names of rabbis who had died hundreds of years before, Shari blurted out, "I don't know who these people were and I don't care! All I care about is if what you are saying makes sense!"

I understood at that moment that true education is the ability to articulate the most important ideas in a way that rings true to the reader's soul from the outset. This is what I have tried to accomplish throughout Life is Great!

As you are reading, when I refer to the Bible, I am referencing the Tanach, which includes the five books of Moses, Prophets and Writings.

When I use the term "Talmud" or "Kabbala," I am referring to different parts of the oral tradition that G-d taught Moses on Mt. Sinai. This oral tradition was subsequently published in different stages in various works between the years 100-500 CE.

When I use the word "Torah" or the term "Ancient Jewish Wisdom," I am referring to the entire scope of Jewish tradition, the written and oral law and authentic commentaries.

Rabbi Yitz Wyne

Life Is Great!

Revealing the 7 Secrets to a More Joyful You!

Especially written for the happy and the soon-to-be happier

Introduction

Life Is Better Than Good—it's *Great!*

How Embracing This Reality Will Change Your Life

WHEN ASKED, MOST people will agree that it is good to be alive. I say that it is *great* to be alive! After going through this book, I am confident that you will have the skills, necessary to appreciate life in all of its glory on a more regular basis.

Happiness is not a selfish or trivial pursuit—it is a very, very important issue. Happier people make the world a better place. They treat themselves and others better. If everyone was happier, marriages would be better, schools would be more effective, and the cost of health care would plummet. There would be a reduction in the size of our police forces, and we wouldn't require as many prisons and probably many armies would disband. Happiness is that powerful.

This book will teach you how to become a happier person and will empower you to make the lives of others better as well.

Happiness is the pleasure one feels when they appreciate that life is good.

Many people feel that if they could only acquire or accomplish certain things, *then* they would be happy. Then there are those who say that a person can be happy for no reason at all. The thinking is that people can just decide to be happy without giving credence to any external circumstance.

Ancient Jewish wisdom rejects both of those notions. Everyone needs to recognize that we all possess a limited amount of talent, money, health, love, and opportunity. Personal happiness is dependent on our ability to appreciate and rejoice over this limited portion.

Chances are, you are probably *pretty* happy with your life. As a general rule, unhappy people don't pick up books on how to be happy, which begs the next question.

Why do happy people need a book on living joyfully?

Like a well-running car, our emotional and spiritual states require periodic servicing and tune-ups. The most successful relationships will always benefit from an occasional "recharge" or "shot in the arm." As a matter of fact, all of life contains peaks and valleys. Sometimes we feel great about life; sometimes we get a little depressed. Most often our emotional state is somewhere in the middle. Our goal is to raise the peaks a little higher and hold on to them a little longer. Make the valleys not so deep and to learn how to pop ourselves out of them more quickly. And finally, lift the general state of being to a more desirable level.

Everyone benefits from *You* living a more joyful life. Studies show that happy people are healthier, live longer, make more money, and have more fulfilling relationships. They have better marriages and are more successful in raising their children. You don't need a study to tell you that you would rather spend time with someone who is happy than someone who is miserable. (Unless of course you are helping the miserable person, in which case you are happier!) I think that anyone would be hard-pressed to find a terrorist or violent criminal who is truly happy. Happy people are into making the world a better place, and everyone benefits from their presence. One of the true litmus tests to know if you are genuinely happy is if you can identify when you are causing others pain, or elevating them and making feel good about their life, and you are doing the latter.

Living joyfully is very attainable. We just need the right combination of wisdom and skills in order to achieve a happier existence. This book will help you unlock the chains that are holding you back.

It will teach you how to give yourself a "tune-up," and recharge your inspiration and clarity.

A great way to find clarity in anything is to ask yourself, "What do I want for my children?"

Even if you don't have children, ask the question and it will make you wiser.

If you are like most people, your answer will be "I want them just to be happy." Happiness is the most obvious answer because the alternative is so horrible! Few things bother parents more than an unhappy child. When children are upset and fight with each other, it causes a very unique, sharp pain to their parents.

A friend of mine, Lionel Ketchin, founder of the *happinessclub.com*, shared the following story with me. When teaching his college course on happiness, he used to begin each class by asking people what is most important in their lives. People would say things like "my family," "success in my career," "my health." He would then ask, "When these things are going well, how does it make you feel?" Invariably people would respond, "It makes me happy."

Lionel would then point out that what everyone really wants is personal happiness. All these things that are important to us are, in actuality, just instruments to help us to feel more joy in life.

Aristotle was quoted as saying, "All things are a means to an end, except for happiness, which is an end unto itself."

Just how happy are you?

When teaching my "Life is Great" seminars, I begin each session by having everyone establish their Happiness Quotients. I ask everyone to rate their personal happiness by ascribing to themselves a number between 1 and 10; '10' representing a state of radiant joy, and '1' representing, a state of near suicidal depression.

This quick and seemingly superficial measure of one's personal happiness has triggered dramatic changes in the lives of countless individuals. Some people realize that their Happiness Quotient is not as high as they would like it to be, and they become driven to do something to pump it up. I have also seen people who feel great about their lives, which their HQ number confirms. This gives people who are already walking the path, a quick reminder of how great their life really is.

There are moments when articulating your happiness quotient in a group could be frustrating because you aren't as happy as you think you should be, or you aren't as happy you think someone else is. I like to call it the "I'm so depressed because I'm not as happy as I should be syndrome".

The truth is that people who are concerned about happiness are often doing much better than they think they are. When I was in rabbinical school in Jerusalem, the head rabbi would often tell us that if we really understood that the Almighty loves us more than we could ever love our own children, we would be in a constant state of exuberance, marveling about how wonderful it is to be alive. My classmates and I were determined to follow our rabbi's advice, so we spent long hours discussing how each of us could 'work' on being happier. It is no small wonder that visitors to school were always deeply impressed and moved by how happy the rabbinic students were.

Recently, after returning from a brief but exhilarating ski vacation with one of my sons, I returned to my synagogue amidst projects and 'crises' that somehow felt more daunting to me than usual. I was also probably a little run-down from the travel and hectic schedule. At the end of my first long day back at work, which I'd spent playing 'catch up' with people, projects and problems, I suddenly remembered that I had to teach a class later that evening. Instead of sharing dinner with my family, I hastily prepared for my classes and attended a *high-intensity* synagogue Board of Directors meeting. By the time I walked into the class that evening, I was quite literally *not myself!* And, when the group of adult students asked me how I was doing, I squeezed my face into something that resembled a smile and responded with, "Pretty good!" I was taken aback when I heard a collective audible gasp of air and saw worried expressions on their faces! They looked stunned and were silent for a few seconds before someone said, "YOU are only 'pretty good?' Rabbi, if YOU are only 'pretty good,' how can we ever even hope to get to 'OK'?"

Happiness ratings are subjective

I started to share a conversation that I had with my brother Richard, who is a member of the Ski Patrol on Blackcomb Mountain in Whistler, British Columbia. He said that they rate the difficulty of ski runs according to color symbols; green for the easiest, blue for an intermediate run, black diamond for the more difficult runs, and so on. Every mountain rates its ski runs by comparing the runs to other runs on that mountain.

So when it comes to his mountain, which is generally more difficult, if the ski run has a green dot rating, I should be prepared for a blue run in another place. When I go on a blue run, I should expect something more similar to a run that would have a black diamond rating on another mountain, a black diamond in Blackcomb, could be like a double diamond in another place, etc.

I explained to the group that when it comes to rating your happiness, the same concept applies. You can only rate your happiness compared to yourself. One person's nine is another person's seven; one person's eight is another person's five. So, don't even bother comparing your Happiness Quotient to someone else's, it really isn't relevant.

Comparing our Happiness Quotient to others can actually distort the process and make it much less valuable. One Passover Seder (dinner), I asked everyone to go around the table and state their Happiness Quotient. There were about thirty people joining us that year and the first person to speak was my 17 year old son Tali. Tali is a happy guy and he enthusiastically said that he was about a 7. Well, the next person didn't want to be thought of as less happy than Tali, so he was an automatic 8. With no one wanting to be out done, soon people were off the scale going to 12 and 14! At the end of the exercise my 14 year old son Aharon exclaimed, "So, what we've learned from all this is that Tali is the most depressed person in the room!

Growing your personal Happiness Quotient is a very meaningful life goal. This book will give you the tools you need in order to work toward and achieve that growth.

Is there anything more important than personal happiness?

In reality, there are more important things in life than being happy. Living a life of goodness and purpose is much dearer to us.

Think of the child who plays video games until the wee hours of the mornings at the expense of his schoolwork; or a teenager who parties incessantly and indulges in his every physical desire. Certainly such a child would claim that these things make him happy.

We will disagree because we know that a truly pleasurable life is achieved through meaningful, moral accomplishments. Even if it made him miserable to put away video games and change his lifestyle, in the end, his life will be more pleasurable and we will insist that he does it.

Why then did I write a book on happiness? Perhaps I should have written one on how to live your life with more meaningful accomplishments? The undeniable truth is that joy and happiness are the fuel to all aspects of greatness. People simply don't continue doing things well in the long run when they are miserable. Even if they aren't miserable, even if they are just okay, their life won't be what it is supposed to be. Intuitively, we all know that we were created for so much more than *okay*.

One of the reasons that the song "I Can't Get No Satisfaction" by the Rolling Stones was so popular, was because almost everyone feels, at times, unsatisfied. King Solomon even discussed how almost everyone dies with less than half of their desires fulfilled. At the same time, intuitively, people know that we were created for pleasure and we should be enjoying life. "Life is great!" is more than a catch phrase, it is a statement of reality.

Dealing with this most basic human conflict is one of the most important and potentially rewarding challenges in life.

When determining the purpose of something, we observe what it does. A pen is a writing instrument because that is what it does. A car is primarily a method of transportation because of how we use it.

What then is the purpose of a human being?

We are pleasure seekers. How much pleasure we get is the principle impetus for every decision we make. As a matter of fact, I don't think I could get you to do anything that wasn't your pleasure. Suppose I forced you to do menial chores that you *hate* doing, under the threat of some horrific punishment. Compared to the punishment, doing the chores would be your *pleasure*! It's not uncommon in life to accept the lesser of two evils with even a tinge of a smile.

One time a friend of mine was teaching this concept in a class and a young man contested the point by saying, "Rabbi, if I want to prove you wrong by taking a knife and slicing up my hand, surly you would not say that that was pleasurable!" My friend responded by saying that it was just more of a pleasure to prove the rabbi wrong than it was for him to have a functional hand.

The other impetus for our decisions is the avoidance of pain. Many people divorce their spouses or scrap life-long aspirations because to succeed at them would require too much effort or pain.

You probably know a lot of people who go to jobs every day that they cannot stand. It is not pleasurable for them to go; however, they need the paycheck. What is behind their decision to keep going into their jobs? It is more "pleasurable" to go to work and have a paycheck than it is to be out of work and be poor.

Point: Our quest for pleasure and avoidance of pain help determine our decisions and, therefore, our personal happiness. Throughout this book, you will learn how to identify and appreciate better all your potential pleasures in order to experience a more enriched life.

What is pleasure?

Pleasure is the emotional feeling one gets when they enjoy an aspect of their lives.

One of the primary reasons pleasure is so valuable is that it is life's fuel. Pleasure gives us energy to truly live and accomplish things important to us.

There is confusion with what pleasure is and what it is not. Most people jumble all their pleasures into a bundle. Even when people experience joyful moments, often they are combined with things that aren't so pleasurable. That makes it difficult to enjoy what they are experiencing.

The following scene was once described to me: Jim was at his friend's wedding, but Jim's mom was bugging him to get married. The food was good, but his suit was too tight. There was plenty of room to dance, but the music was too loud; and even though his date was gorgeous, he was constantly annoyed because two other guys kept hitting on her. Such confusion!

This could have been a great party for him, but it wasn't. Even though there was plenty of good, there was also plenty of bad in the evening. Because everything was all mixed up together, it was too difficult for Jim to focus on what he could have enjoyed. In order to really enjoy life, we need to use our minds to segregate and prioritize our emotions and pleasures.

We can take all life's pleasures and categorize them into five categories or classes. However, there is also with each class a counterfeit pleasure. A counterfeit pleasure is something that I assume is pleasurable but, when left unchecked, will lead to the proverbial pleasure train wreck at the end of the tunnel. Marrying someone because you think you are in love but you really are infatuated is an example of this.

I will discuss this in more detail later in Secret # 6. But for now, understand that if you know which pleasures are available, you are more likely to experience them. Happy people seem to have an innate ability to focus on the pleasure they are experiencing at a particular time and just enjoy it. We will learn how to do this.

If people want true pleasure, then what is the problem? We should be living in an almost utopian society where everyone is walking on cloud nine!

The problem is that people make mistakes. Some are small; some are large. It is those mistakes that knock us off the track of living a truthfully joyful life.

Stick with this book, and you will find out what mistakes most people make and how to avoid them. When you stumble, and everyone stumbles sometimes, you will learn how to positively deal with and rectify your mistakes. In the process, you will become a happier, more joyful person. You will have better relationships, a more prosperous career, and a more satisfying life in general!

Secret # 1

Clarity or Death!

Finding Your Bottom Line

MY MENTOR AND teacher, Rabbi Noah Weinberg of blessed memory, would often proclaim, "Clarity or death!" There are few moments of joy, like the joy of being absolutely clear and directed in knowing what you are doing.

When it comes to being happy, it is especially important to know what you are talking about.

The truth is, you should always know what you are talking about, whether you are talking about happiness or any important issue in life.

Mean what you say and say what you mean!

The most fundamental point of any conversation is to ensure that each person understands the other. We do this best by defining our terms.

How many times have you said to someone, or someone said to you, "I love you"? Who hasn't wondered what exactly did he or she mean by that? What did you mean by that? I have personally counseled many married couples and individuals over the years, who could have avoided tremendous and often debilitating emotional pain if, *before* plunging into romantic relationships, they had honestly clarified what "love" really meant to them.

Winston Churchill was once quoted as saying, "I didn't have time to write a short speech, so I wrote a long one instead."

If one of the greatest orators of the past century could make fun of his tendency to over-speak, how much more so should the rest of us take care to measure our words.

Being succinct is difficult because it requires us to define our terms and measure our words. Often, we can do this simply by identifying what we want to communicate before we speak.

There is a story about a man who approaches a rabbi following a one-hour sermon on "Love thy neighbor." The man introduced himself as a television producer, "Rabbi, the concepts you spoke about were so brilliant, I would like to put you on television so you could share them with the whole world. However, the air time is so expensive. Tell me, is it possible for you to articulate everything you said in five minutes?" The rabbi says, "Sure!" The man quipped "Then why didn't you?"

While being verbose might seem impressive, it often clouds the issues and creates confusion.

What is better, clarity or brilliance?

If you are reading this book, you probably value wisdom and appreciate educated people. You have a drive toward personal growth and want to be the best that you can be at everything. These are wonderful and worthwhile goals . . . as long as they accompany clarity.

Without clarity in the most important aspects of our lives, all the erudition, intellectual superiority, and accomplishment, will not bring us the happiness and fulfillment we are seeking.

Understand that more important than brilliance is clarity. Clarity about life; clarity about our values, clarity about what we want. After we have achieved this, we will be ready to experience a more joyful existence.

I am going to show you how to develop clarity about the most important things to you. That in itself will lead you to a more peaceful, happier state of mind. Afterward, I will show you how to apply these principles to living a more joyful, happier life.

Before we begin, understand that you recognize truth when you see it. There is an ancient Jewish teaching that when we are in our mother's womb, an angel is sent from G-d to teach us everything we need to know about life. What is right and what is wrong, how to be happy, how to love—everything! Then immediately before we are born, the angel touches us underneath the nose and we forget all that we have learned.

Why would an angel tell us everything we need to know and then make us forget before we can even use it?!"

The seeds of our intuition are those pieces of wisdom that the angel taught us. The process of life's journeys includes a rediscovering of these truths. The brilliance behind this teaching is that life is not a journey where we are struggling to learn new things; it is a process we go through to rediscover what we already know.

How can we rediscover these truths?

Pay attention to the world around you and keep asking yourself, "What is the message in this event for me?" Learning to listen to the quiet voice inside of you is the key to getting in touch with your intuition.

If you want to take this concept a step further, consider the following. Ancient Jewish wisdom teaches that in life there are no accidents. Every situation is an opportunity to learn new lessons and deepen our understanding about life. As Rabbi Weinberg often told me, "The Almighty is always communicating with us and He is a very articulate teacher!" For many, asking themselves "What does G-d want me to do in this particular situation?" is often enough to stir their inner conscience and moral guide. Clarity in life requires us to trust our perceptions and intuition.

Who is considered wise?

The Talmudic sages have answered that question with "one who learns from everyone." I have made it a priority to learn from my experiences with everyone I come into contact with, in order to develop wisdom and share it with others.

As a rabbi, I encounter many different kinds of people with various challenges. One such fellow was Todd. When we met, he was a good-looking, professional twenty-six-year-old man beginning a promising career. Unfortunately, he was also in a constant state of emotional pain. He used to say, "My parents always told me to go to college and get a master's degree, so I did. But they never told me why. They never told me what my life was about, and I just can't figure it out!"

Could you really blame them for not properly directing their son? They were probably not clear about their own inner values, let alone having clarity about what they would wish for their son. In our society, it is very common for people to spend years thinking, dreaming, and educating themselves on how to make a living, but very little time discussing how to prepare for marriage, parenting, or how to be a good friend. What is remarkable is that most people would agree that in terms of priorities; marriage, parenting, and friendship, would come before making more money. However, in practical terms, these things are often pushed onto a back burner to be addressed at a later time, if they are addressed at all.

Todd's education helped him make a living, but it fell short of teaching him how to have a life. Sadly, he is not alone.

Just to illustrate the point, would you rather be happy or rich? Not that they are mutually exclusive, but certainly it would be foolish to chase after one while completely neglecting the other.

Getting our priorities straight

What is the most important question you can ask yourself?
—What am I living for?

If you have a good answer for this question, "What am I living for?", it will affect many decisions you make throughout the day. If not, your life can be as directionless as a boat at sea without a sail or rudder. You will be tossed in whatever direction the prevailing tide is going.

One time, when giving a class, I went around the room and asked everyone to share what they are living for. Only five out of eighteen people gave an answer and only three of the answers were real, truthful, and relevant.

Stacy gave the answer that would lead to the most enriched life: "I'm living to make the world a better place."

Fantastic! At the end of every day, Stacy can ask herself if she made a material difference in people's lives that day. Did she smile, encourage, and empower others? Was she kind and productive? Stacy has clarity in life, and over the years, she will be able to reflect and enjoy her contributions to the world.

The problem is that we aren't really trained or ever encouraged to ask the question. There is no "life goals" channel on television. Your boss probably won't encourage you to think about them on the job; there is no obvious connection between clear life goals and your capacity to earn a heftier salary. It is actually the opposite. Imagine spotting one of your employees sitting at his desk, not working on his assigned project. You ask him, "What are you doing?" And he replies, "Oh, just trying to figure out what to do with my life." Your response will probably be something like, "Not on my dime, buddy. Get back to work!"

Knowing what we are living for plays a major role in our personal happiness, ability to live joyfully, and feel that life is good. Later in Secret # 7 we will discover exciting and practical strategies on how to further clarify and answer that question for ourselves.

As Rabbi Noah Weinberg always said, "Clarity or death!" Confusion and ignorance are the most virulent diseases in the world. If people don't know what they are living for, they won't know and appreciate the purpose and meaning of their life. This will cause them to make decisions that in the end will waste away their days, if not years. In the most extreme cases, it could lead a person to cause untold pain to others or even take his own life. Divorce, drug addiction, alienation—these are all products of confusion and ignorance.

Sometimes the smartest people are the most confused. In rabbinical school, they used to say, "Asking the question is more than half the answer!". Mind you, this only applies if one really wants an answer. I've met people with doctorate degrees who ask and ask and ask. In the end only to trip themselves and others up in their own logic.

How do you find out what you are living for?

As obvious as it sounds, the best way to find answers is to ask questions. The difficulty is to know which questions to ask. In terms of clarifying the ultimate purpose for your life, ask questions that will sift away the minor goals, desires, and aspirations for the more meaningful and significant ones.

What are you willing to die for?

Perhaps your family, country, religious, or moral beliefs . . .

In Judaism we believe that unless you know what you are willing to die for, you have not yet begun to live. Whereas it may be true that we never really know if we would be willing to give our life for something until the moment arrives, being committed, even if it is only on an intellectual level, will give you real direction on where to invest your time and energy.

Realize that if you are willing to die for something, you should be willing to live for it.

It is time to take a moment and begin the personal exploration of what it means to live for your most treasured values.

David was a really nice guy who was having some terrible problems in his marriage. He and his wife felt that over the years they had simply grown apart. In an effort to help him clarify his values and true purpose in life, I asked him what he was willing to die for. His response was a quick, confident "My family, my country, and my religion." Initially, the alacrity of his response took me by surprise, almost as much surprise as it took his wife. However, upon quick reflection of what David did for a living, he was a politician; I realized that he had already thought about how to verbalize an answer to that question.

It was my next question that caused him discomfort. "Okay, you are willing to die for your family, country, and religion. What actions do you perform that show you are willing to live for these things?"

Thoughts and intentions are great, but ultimately, it is our actions that define who and what we are. If David's actions reflected his answer to the question, his wife never would have dragged him to my office. That is why she was so surprised to hear that he would die for his family. There were very few actions that she saw, which represented that value.

By the way, if something is worth dying for, and it is worth living for, then it is certainly worth enjoying!

my Family
pay my Bills
Israel

To experience this more:

- Identify the three most important things in your life.
- Commit to the performance of one action every day that illustrates your values to others.
- Make a decision to find ways to living your values them more.

What do you really want for your life?

If you are having trouble figuring out what you should be living for, try identifying and listing your life goals.

A life goal is something that if you *did not* fulfill, you would have a great sense of disappointment.

They don't need to be heavy or philosophical . . . but they do need to be specific. "Being a good person" is very noble but too vague. Rather, it is more helpful if you say things like: "Try always to do the right thing" or "try to cheer up every person I meet"

Afterward, assign a number value to each goal signifying how important it is to you.

What is getting in the way of you fulfilling these goals?

This question often really trips people up. A natural temptation is to blame other people or situations for things that are out of our control. Joyful people end up taking responsibility for their lives and major accomplishments.

7 times the righteous man falls and gets up,
the wicked only falls once.

—King Solomon from Proverbs 24:16

Judaism has a very interesting approach to righteousness. The righteous man is not the individual who never makes mistakes because *everyone* makes mistakes. The righteous person is the one who keeps getting up and trying to do better. The wicked man only falls once because he doesn't bother getting back up.

Do you value partial accomplishments or only complete achievements?

Something is always better than nothing—if the something is real. One pitfall is the "all or nothing" myth. This is the confusion that unless I am able to do everything, it isn't worth doing anything.

Imagine a person who wanted to travel the world but could only get one month off from work. How foolish would it be for him not to go anywhere because he couldn't go everywhere! Joyful people understand that one month is a twelfth of a year, and it is still a significant accomplishment. So we would tell that person, "Take that trip! Something is better than nothing, you will have a great month!" As a friend of mine once said, "How do you eat an elephant? One bite at a time!"

"Every journey begins with a single step" is a very real spiritual principle. Also, it is a practical way to deal with life's most difficult problems, and an effective strategy to conquer our most grandiose goals.

When I have a problem that is tough to solve, I break it down into as many small problems as possible. If I am able to solve two of the ten, then my *big* problem is now 20 percent smaller and a lot easier to face.

If I have an ambitious goal, I take the same approach; and similar to taking a hatchet to a redwood, eventually the tree comes falling down!

What questions should you ask to find clarity?

First and foremost, clarity requires definitions.

As we alluded to before, how many times have you told someone you were dating "I love you"? Do you really know what love is? How would you define love? *Can* you define love? How do you tell someone you love them if you can't define the word? Or maybe it's one of those things for which you can't come up with a real definition, but when you see it, you know what it is.

What about the concept of friendship? What do you mean by a friend? Is a friend just someone to hang around with? Maybe a true friend needs to be loyal and a source of support and enrichment. We may have some nebulous, vague ideas of what we mean, but if we don't have concrete definitions, we are in dangerous territory.

Anyone who uses words and concepts without knowing what they mean is, at best, on a slope to lousy communication, arguments, and confusion. Even worse, it can lead to an abuse of language that can have horrible effects on people's lives.

One of the most listened-to radio personalities, a famous shock jock, used to play a clip of himself, as a ten year old, telling a joke on his father's radio program. After the joke, his father shouts at the boy calling him a stupid moron. For years, he claimed (or joked) that it was his father's fault that he spent so much time on a psychiatrist's couch!

I don't know if this was the case with this celebrity's father, but as strange as it sounds, I know parents who deeply care for their children and use degrading nicknames as terms of endearment.

The Bible teaches us that G-d created the universe with words. This sends a message that language, if used properly, is an instrument of creation. If not used properly, it can be a tool of untold destruction. In Jewish consciousness, malicious gossip is considered worse than murder, idolatry, and adultery!

If a person called you a *bafufstick*, would you receive it as an insult or a compliment? It all depends on how you define *bafufstick*.

When it comes to happiness and joy, we need to be very clear on what we are talking about.

How do you define happiness?

Happiness is the emotional pleasure one feels when they appreciate that life is good. It is created when we focus on what we have.

How do you define joy?

Joy is the emotion one experiences when they anticipate future good.

On the simplest level, when we focus on what is good about our lives, we are happy. When we focus on our troubles, we become miserable.

When we look forward to upcoming special events, we become filled with energy, life, and joy.

Sounds too simple?

The most profound concepts in life are often not difficult to understand, just difficult to do. By the time you finish this book, you will know how to acquire and implement the ability to focus on what is great about your life, and look forward to what lies ahead.

My rabbi and mentor, Noah Weinberg of blessed memory, told me the story of how one time he was visited by a young man, Sam, with an unusually happy disposition. The rabbi asked Sam, "What's your secret? How did you become so happy?"

Sam said, "When I was eleven years old, G-d gave me a gift of happiness. I was riding my bicycle when a strong gust of wind blew me onto the ground, into the path of an oncoming truck. The truck ran over me and cut off my leg.

As I lay there bleeding, I thought to myself, I might have to live the rest of my life without a leg. I was immediately depressed! After a few moments, I realized that being depressed won't get my leg back. So I decided right then and there not to waste my life being upset over my loss.

When I woke up in the hospital, my parents were standing over me, all shocked and grieving. My father said to me, 'Son, you've lost a leg. It's horrible, but you are going to have to get used to this.' I remember telling them, 'Actually, Dad, Mom, you are the ones who will have to get used to this. I already am.'

Ever since then, I began to see my friends getting upset over little things: their bus came late, they got a bad grade on a test, and somebody insulted them. I just enjoy life."

At age eleven, Sam attained the clarity that focusing on what he is missing is a waste of time, a waste of his life. He also understood that he chooses what to focus on and what to ignore.

This is the ultimate secret to happiness—taking pleasure in what you have.

When I was twenty years old, I was the best man at my friend's wedding. It was a very large, ritzy affair at the Helmsly Palace in New York City. During the party, I saw the mother of the bride, all stressed-out, running around barking orders at the hotel staff. I stopped her and said, "Mrs. Stein, are you having a good time?" She paused for a moment, allowed a smile to slowly grace her face, and replied, "Yes, yes, I am, thank you."

This was the wedding of her only daughter! An amazing affair that was probably one of the best days of her life; but she forgot to enjoy it, until I reminded her.

We need to, and will, learn how to identify our pleasures and not forget to experience them.

> **If you want to experience this more:**
>
> - Think of a time in your life when you should have been enjoying things immensely, but got distracted by other things and you missed your chance to enjoy.
> - Make a decision to focus on the pleasure you can experience right now.

Why don't we focus on our pleasures?

The truth is, every one of us makes the mistake of getting distracted and not focusing on our pleasures. I call it the *universal craziness*. It is universal because there is no one who is immune. It is crazy because when we recognize it, we see how ridiculous it is. Imagine driving down the highway and throwing five-dollar bills out the window. That is crazy! You worked hard for that money and now you are just throwing it away without benefiting from it. When we spend effort trying to have pleasure and then, for what ever reason, we miss it, we are doing the exact same thing. Paying for something in effort, without receiving the benefit.

I remember an incident when one of my young children was behaving in a super-cute fashion. I was oodiling over him with my father and asked my dad if I did the same thing when I was four years old. (I happen to know that I was a very cute kid growing up!)

My dad responded with an extremely disappointing and sobering remark. He said, "I don't remember. I always thought I was around when you kids were growing up, but even though I was there physically, I guess my mind was somewhere else."

Shortly after this conversation I saw the movie *Click* starring Adam Sandler. In the movie, he plays a character that literally misses his family growing up. He was there physically, but his mind became accustomed to being somewhere else. I thought to myself, "Wow, if I'm not careful, that could become me!"

I made a personal commitment not to make the same mistake as my father did; and yes, like my father, I struggle every day with it.

Practice, Practice, Practice makes almost perfect

When my kids were younger and just learning to play basketball, I used to tell them that I could get Kobe Bryant to show them how to make a free throw. However, it wouldn't really help unless they were willing to practice making two hundred shots everyday for a month. As with most skills, the skill of living with joy can be revealed and taught over pretty simply, but it takes practice to master.

What prevents us from taking one of the most valuable skills we ever could learn and practicing it until we master it?

—We are crazy!

The reality is that we are all a little crazy. It is this craziness that prevents us from achieving clarity. Therefore, the battle for life is a struggle with insanity. Recognizing this, we are ahead of the game.

There is a story told of a king who one day was approached by his advisers. They frantically informed the monarch that all the grain supplies in the kingdom had become contaminated. Anyone who would eat the grain would become insane. However, the good news was that there was enough "good" grain remaining to feed the royal court.

The king commanded his advisers to have everyone at court tattoo a mark on their foreheads and eat the contaminated grain along with everyone else. When the advisers asked the king why they should do such a thing, he explained, "If we eat the good grain and don't seem crazy like everyone else, my subjects may think that we are crazy and overthrow us. Therefore, we must eat the same grain and suffer the same insanity as everyone else, except we have one advantage. Every time we look at each other and see the marks on our foreheads, we will *know* we're crazy!"

Recognizing that we often have great pleasures at our fingertips, but get too distracted to enjoy them, will help us snap into a happier state when we remember this. In Secret # 6, I will reveal tools you can use that will help you truly appreciate and focus on your pleasures more frequently.

The clearest person I have ever met was Rabbi Noah Weinberg. He told a story of himself growing up in New York. He was nine years old, and one day, his entire class had decided to play hooky and go to the 1939 World's Fair. There was one condition to join the group. Everyone had to pay their own way, which amounted to $1. He was broke and so was the rest of his family. Therefore he decided to just go to school. On his way to school, he began to daydream about finding the money. Before long, he was praying to the Almighty to find just $1. Next, he began "bargaining" with G-d ("G-d, if You will let me find a dollar, I promise not to fight with my sister anymore," etc.) The promises got bigger and bigger, and he really wanted to go to the fair, until finally, his promises reached the height of all promises. "Please, G-d, if you will let me find a dollar, I promise I'll never do anything wrong for the rest of my life!" Then he began to laugh. He came to the realization that eludes most people nine times his age. He realized that if he found his precious dollar, he would promptly skip school to attend the World's Fair! *That's clarity*!

Clarity demands that we are honest with ourselves. As long as we allow life's illusions and misconceptions to hang on to our thoughts, we won't be able to make the decisions that will allow us to live really joyfully.

Points to remember:

- Clarity in life requires us to trust our perceptions and intuition.
- Use definitions.
- Happiness is the emotion you have when you focus on the good in your life.
- It is crazy to get distracted from enjoying your pleasures.
- If you know you are crazy, you can do something about it.
- Clarity demands that we are honest with ourselves.

Your Notes

Secret # 2

Choosing Joy:

Making It Your Driving Force

Now that we know what our lives are about, and we have a working definition of happiness, the most important point of living joyfully is wanting to do it.

It sounds strange, but it is all part of the *universal craziness*. We spend so much time being involved in our lives; getting an education, building a career, getting into/out of relationships that we forget what we really want is a deep sense of happiness. People don't try *not* to be happy; life just has so many demands. With the pressures of making a living, raising the children, staying healthy and keeping physically fit, it is often just too difficult to focus on what we really want—happiness.

Is it really in my power to be joyful?

When it comes to personal growth, nothing stands in the way of a person's will. The Kabbalah teaches, "In the way a person wishes to go, they shall lead him!"

The Talmud explains that the "they" refers to angels. The Almighty assesses what we truly want and creates spiritual forces to help us achieve those desires. Whether it is for good or for bad, our fortune is largely set on what we truly want. That is why it is so important to be in touch with what you want; G-d is always helping you along the way in paths you might not even recognize.

Therefore, it is especially important to keep focused on the goal of living a happy life.

There is a Jewish legend about a man who, while visiting the Holy Temple in Jerusalem two thousand years ago, eavesdropped on another when he was praying. The man was crying to the Lord, saying, "G-d, please, please let me marry such and such a woman!"

A year later, the same snoop heard the same man praying again except this time he was saying, "G-d, please, make me die or her die, but one of us has to go!"

The lesson: Be careful with what you want and what you pray for. You just might get it!

How you can create a myriad of angels to help you with your goals—any goals—will be discussed in the upcoming "secrets."

Is there anything you have in your life to be happy about right now?

There is an infinite number of pathways to happiness. Just think of all the things in your life that bring you joy. When a person makes the decision to be happy and commitments to living a joyful life, the possibilities are endless. Each moment holds within it the potential of enormous blessing. Because our lives are so complex, that only adds to the areas of potential sources of happiness. We have our health (physical and spiritual); our relationships with family, friends, coworkers, spouses and children; our professional life. The list goes on and on. Every area of our lives contains many opportunities for joy if we so choose.

Happiness is a choice

While we will probably never have complete control over our emotions, we have a lot more than most people think. Our thoughts often control our emotions, and we to a great degree control our thoughts.
Your ability to live joyfully is not dependent on anyone else. No one can "make you" happy or "make you" sad. The most others can do is create situations and environments that make it easier for you to be happy or upset, but ultimately, the choice will be yours.

What happens if someone hurts us?

There are those moments in our lives when situations or people seem to attack us. We could be the subject of intense wickedness that literally could rob us of our will to live. The temptation in these cases is to give ourselves a pass on choosing to be happy. One could say, "I've suffered so much, how could I possibly be happy? I will simply live out my life in misery."

This is one of the most pernicious tools of the "evil inclination." The evil inclination is a power that was created by G-d and placed near our souls. Its purpose is to tempt us to do the wrong thing, thereby creating the dynamic of free will. It is symbolized in the Bible as the snake who tempted Adam and Eve to eat from the forbidden fruit in the Garden of Eden.

Regarding the evil inclination, the Talmud teaches, that it rises every day with the intention of killing us. Free will is not the choice between chocolate ice cream and vanilla—that is preference. It is not even the choice between good and evil. *Everyone* chooses to be good—even the most evil, immoral people like Hitler, Osama Bin Laden, and Mahmoud Ahmadinejad, justify their actions so that in their minds they would be doing good.

Ultimately, free will is the choice between life and death. That is why in the Bible it says, "I have put before you, life and death . . . Choose life so that you may live" (Deuteronomy 30:19).

The evil inclination probably won't convince you to jump in front of a truck, but it might have you sleep in an extra ten minutes when you don't need the rest. It probably won't convince you to overdose on heroin, but it might be successful at having you constantly think about the people who have caused you harm. Either way you have been robbed of your life.

You know it is the evil inclination when, at the end of the day, you have not made progress on your life goals, when you have not contributed to making the world a better place.

Focusing on how others have harmed you is like ingesting poison and expecting it to hurt the other guy. He probably doesn't even know you are thinking of him. If he does, he probably doesn't care or is glad that you are wasting your life.

When we give in to the trickery of the evil inclination, the ones who are most hurt are ourselves. When we are able to rise above the evil inclination, do what is right, live our lives productively and choose happiness, our rewards are very great.

Immediately we are filled with a greater sense of self-respect, confidence, and strength. Jewish tradition teaches that this is the primary way to earn a more splendid eternity in heaven or, as Jews call it, "the world to come."

Most events and situations in life are beyond our control. What *is* in our control is our attitude toward them. In "Secret # 4: Focusing on the Good," we will discuss in greater detail how to evaluate events in a positive light, which will deeply affect our emotions.

However, for now, we need to accept that even though we cannot control the hand of cards that life deals us, we can control how that hand is played.

Our initial impression of every one of life's events falls into one of three categories; either we view them as positive, negative, or neutral.

With few exceptions, life's events are in actuality almost all exclusively neutral. We, however, make a choice, almost unconsciously, to evaluate them as positive or negative.

Two people get laid off from their jobs; one person spends his days in emotional anxiety over how he will pay the mortgage, and the other takes extra time that he now has available, and spends it with his family.

King Solomon wrote in Proverbs, "The Almighty created man straightforward, but they invented many calculations." The "many calculations" refer to the enemies of happiness. We create a lot of our own frustration, dissatisfaction, and misery. This is the primary tool of the evil inclination. These "calculations" can lead to depression, which is the ultimate thief of our lives.

The truth is that every event in life can be interpreted for the good and for the bad. A twelve-ounce glass that contains six ounces of water is both half-empty and half-full at the same time. How you relate to that glass is up to you. To some people, the glass is always half-empty; to some people, the glass is always half-full. For most people, it is sometimes this way and sometimes that way.

Not only do we have the ability to control our emotions but we also can change the direction of our emotional outlook on a dime.

Have you ever noticed a person who was very upset and scolded a family member; then all of a sudden, a stranger showed up at the door, and they amazingly became very nice and pleasant? This is an example of someone's mind quickly changing their mood to something more beneficial to them.

A friend of mine, Nathan, explained to me how he learned this lesson. He was once waiting tables in a restaurant where the kitchen staff was unusually incompetent. It seemed the only way for the servers to get their orders taken care of quickly was to yell and scream at the cooks. Of course, he had to be charming and pleasant to the customers at the tables. There was a swinging door that everyone would kick open in order to enter and exit the kitchen. He realized that his mood would change with the kick of the door. One moment he would be pleasant and charming and the next, ferocious. Why? Because he had to be!

You see, on some level, we already exert control over emotions, when we need to. The trick is to choose to be happier when we don't necessarily feel the need. You will learn how to train yourself to see your cup as half-full in "Secret # 4: Focusing on the Good."

Recognize that the choice of happiness is yours. What do you want to do?

There is a wonderful story about a sassy sixth-grade boy who was always trying to outsmart the teacher in front of his friends. One day, he caught a butterfly in his hands, gathered his friends, and said to the teacher, "Mr. Teacher, I have in my hands a butterfly. If you can guess correctly whether it is alive or dead, then I will behave the whole week. But if you are wrong, then we get extra ten minutes of recess." All the time he was thinking, *If the teacher says dead, I will let the butterfly fly away from my hands. And if the teacher says alive, I could crush the bug in my palms.* The teacher looked at the boy's hands and said, "Son, I'm afraid that whether that butterfly is alive or dead, the answer lies in your hands."

Living joyfully? The answer lies in your hands.

If you want to experience this more:

- Ask yourself, what or who is getting in my way of living a happier life?
- Resolve not to blame it or them but to take personal responsibility for your own happiness and joy.

More than just a choice, it is an obligation!

America's founding fathers wrote about the "pursuit of happiness." That it is one of a few "*unalienable rights*." This means that because no person gave you the right to be happy, no person can take it away from you. However, you do have free will and you can always choose to direct your emotions. It is up to you to choose whether or not to pursue happiness.

I offer an amendment to this concept. Beyond it being a "right," it is the most basic moral obligation of every human being to actively be involved in the pursuit of happiness.

When we live in a state of lethargy, not pursuing joy, we are living immorally. It is as if we are spreading an infectious disease, making it socially acceptable not to be happy. When we allow ourselves to stay in a lousy mood, it is worse than body odor, causing discomfort to everyone we come into contact with. Somehow, many people think that it is their own prerogative to be happy or not.

The Bible teaches that when G-d created man and put him in the Garden of Eden, he was told to work and guard the garden. As if to say, "Adam, here is your world. Now take care of it." It is the most basic responsibility of every human being to make the world a better place. Before we go to sleep at night, we must be able to say that in the past waking hours we somehow contributed to the building and perfecting of the world.

Aside from wisdom, the most important tool we have to make the world better is our ability to live joyfully. Living with happiness and joy gives us the energy and focus to do what we need to do. It allows our vision to expand and, in short, makes us more giving, kinder, and less selfish human beings.

Happiness is an obligation in three different spheres of our lives. It is an obligation to others, it is an obligation to ourselves, and it is an obligation to our Creator.

Happiness is an obligation to others

We generally do not like to be around people who are unhappy, and neither do most of the people we know. Just ask a child who grew up with an unhappy parent about their experience, and you will understand exactly what I'm talking about.

If you want your spouse or children to be happy, don't think that it can happen if you enter your home each day angry, moping, yelling, and frustrated. Your mood will affect them. Have you ever been in a good mood and someone who walks in the room was just miserable and angry? It just bursts your balloon. One minute you are happy and joyful; then they lob a few complaints about their life or unfairly criticize you and ruin your whole day.

Mind you, we shouldn't be; and we will learn how not to be, so susceptible to other people's moods. Rather realize that just as we can be the victims of misery, so too we can also be the cause of it. We owe it to our spouses, children, coworkers, and even the people we casually come into contact with to have a happy disposition.

There is also an altruistic aspect to this. Happy people do more good in the world than those that are unhappy. When you are feeling good about life, you naturally want to help others feel good. If you are happy and hear that something positive happened to a friend, you feel grateful for them. Think of the happiest people you know and how they respond to situations in their lives. Happiness makes us expansive, creative, and charitable.

Conversely, when you think of those who have done the most harm to the world; Nazis, Communists and terrorists, they are not from the happiest groups of people. These are people who are motivated by hatred, misery, and fear. Unsurprisingly enough, that is what they create.

I'm not saying that we should be a bunch of frauds, constantly masking our misery, faking being happy and not having real relationships. On the contrary, the more real and intimate our relationships are, the easier it is for us to be happier. I'm talking about the requirement to make a consistent effort to be joyful and to lift people's spirits.

Bob was a professional actor—and a good one at that—in one of the Las Vegas shows. He was attending the Joyful Living Club and told me that no matter how depressed or angry he was, he could pass himself off as the happiest person in the world. No one would ever suspect otherwise. He felt that he was being hypocritical by behaving happily when he wasn't. Faking it for money on a stage where he would sing and dance was one thing, but around his friends? What kind of friend would he be if he was always masking his feelings and putting up a false front? And what kind of friends would they be if he couldn't be his natural, depressed, and miserable self around them?

I explained that it wasn't an issue of being false. He wasn't supposed to *act* happy; he was supposed to *be* happy! By changing his state of mind and focusing on what is good about his life at that moment, he would lift his spirits, be genuinely more joyful, and in the process, make everyone's day better.

"We are as happy as we decide to be."

—*Abraham Lincoln*

The Talmud takes it a step further to say that "A man's emotions are pulled after his actions." In other words, the happier you act, the happier you will feel. We think that our actions should represent our feelings or at least be determined by our feelings. But according to Jewish tradition, our feelings respond to our behavior. How we act influences our feelings more than our feelings should be allowed to influence our behavior.

Everyone has moments when they need to cry and sulk. But the key word here is *moments*, not months or years—moments.

There are definitely specific times in life that we need to mourn. Our ability to recognize our losses and deal with our pain is crucial to becoming a complete person. Transitional moments in life are often painful. This is one of the reasons why when an immediate relative dies, Jewish law instructs us to take an entire week and mourn intensely. We don't go to work or even shower during that time.

There is even a national day of mourning, the ninth day of the Hebrew month of Av. This is when we focus on all of the suffering that the Jewish people have endured throughout the years. It is preceded by three weeks when Jewish law states that we "reduce our joyfulness." (Note: even when in a state of mourning, we only reduce our joyfulness, not eliminate it completely!)

The Talmud explains that if one is unable to mourn when they need to, they won't have the capacity to rejoice properly when they have the opportunity. Therefore, it is imperative that we become very real with our emotions. At the same time, we must be careful not to extend our sadness beyond the time that it is beneficial to us.

If you can't do it for your own sake, be happy for the sake of others!

"Do it for the children" is such a great cliché because it is a true concept. There are many things in life that we won't do for ourselves, but we will do for others, especially our children.

My mother knew for years that it was wrong to smoke but never really tried to quit. It was only after my sister organized an *almost* "peaceful" rebellion that we persuaded my mom to quit. Afterward, she, of course, would almost gloat, saying that she gave up smoking for the sake of her kids. The truth is that she should have quit for herself. It is just that often we care more about others than we do for ourselves.

One of my students owns a real estate development company and was debating whether to cash out and retire at the tender age of fifty or embark upon another several-year project. He didn't need the money and didn't want the stress. In the end, he continued building because he felt responsible to teach his son the business, just like his father had done for him.

I once received a call on my radio show from a woman who was lamenting that her husband of many years was always grumpy. Even when his job was going well, the family had their health, and there was nothing particular to complain about, he always found a way to scowl. He was very responsible in many areas; and in a strange way, she found him charming. Because of this, she was willing to put up with her husband's grumpiness. However, when she saw the effect that his attitudes were having on their children, she became really bothered. They were growing up to become negative and grumpy like their father. She became conflicted on whether or not to stick with her marriage because the pain of raising unhappy children was becoming too much to bear. It is difficult to raise a happy household if we are not happy ourselves. And as this man came to realize, the cost of allowing oneself to remain unhappy is usually much higher than we ever anticipate.

One of the biggest mistakes people make on a daily basis is coming home after a hard day's work and *not* making everyone there feel like a million bucks. Believe me, they probably have also had a stressful day. Walking in the door with an energetic smile and a compliment can make a whole evening go well for the entire family.

A rabbi of mine used to advise his students to bring an apple home from work every day, and eat it immediately before going into the house. This way they can focus on their wife and kids and not fall into the "What's for dinner?" trap right away.

One time, one of my friends went home, flopped on the couch, and turned on the TV. His wife asked how his day was, and he told her he couldn't talk because he was just too tired. She said that she had something important to discuss with him about the kids, and again he said he was just too tired.

Then the phone rang; she answered it and handed it to her husband, telling him who it was. He energetically popped up from the couch, took the phone, and spoke, "Hey, John, how are you?"

"I'm fantastic!"

"Of course, I'll be over right away! See you in ten minutes! Looking forward to it!"

As he was about to leave the house, he felt his wife's glare. He turned to her and asked, "Am I in trouble?" She replied, "No, it's just now I know how you will be greeting *me* every time you come home!"

Smart woman!

You see, your family is your most important client. A happy wife is a happy life, and a happy spouse is a happy house. It all starts with you, even before you walk through the front door.

The same applies at the office. There are some employers who march through the halls barking and yelling, trying to keep the fear level up in their companies. There is a word for that. It is called being cruel. If you are having a stressful day, what purpose is there in making others suffer? In the end of your life, how do you want to be thought of? As the person who inflicted pain to everyone in your path, exposing all to the wrath of your personal stress, or the one who brought a joyous light to those you touched? There are many successful business people who are kind and friendly and who create an enjoyable work environment.

As infectious as misery is, so is happiness. People who live joyfully leave a feel-good imprint upon everyone they come in contact with. When you do it enough, people will associate the feeling of happiness with you. They will think of you and smile. One of the most meaningful compliments I ever received was given to me when I was nineteen years old, studying in Jerusalem. A person whom I really looked up to, who eventually became a close friend and is now a rabbi in Toronto, asked me for fifteen minutes a day. I agreed and asked why. He told me he needed me for his daily "happiness pill."

Most people are slightly shocked when I share with them the answer to the following question: "There are 613 commandments in the

Bible, the Torah (ten famous ones, but that is for another time). Of all the commandments, which one is the most important?"

There are always good suggestions: Don't murder, don't steal, and honor your parents; even love your neighbor often works its way into the list of possible answers.

According to Judaism, the most important commandment is to learn the Torah. It is only by learning the Torah that we will be able to fulfill all the other commandments. This is why the Talmud tells us that "the learning of Torah is equivalent to all of the other commandments combined."

And where is the commandment to learn the Torah found in the Bible? It isn't! The Bible only says that one must "teach the Torah to your children." In other words, the most important commandment in the Bible is articulated as an obligation to our children.

I know from personal experience that if I am learning something by myself and I'm not so clear on the point, I might just continue on to the next paragraph. However, if I have to teach it to someone else, especially if that someone else is one of my own children, I will go over and over the material until it is crystal clear.

If we truly view happiness as an obligation to others, we will be motivated and inspired to get it right! The result will be that our lives will be filled with joy and energy.

If you want to experience this more:

- Identify a few people whose happiness is important to you.
- Ask yourself, "How should I behave around them so they can be happier?"
- Next time you are in their presence, implement those behaviors.

Emails + Telephone

Happiness is an obligation to ourselves

Every person knows intuitively that they must try to have the best life they can. When it comes to our physical health, the Bible even commands us to guard our soul. Studies have shown that happy people are healthier and they accomplish more than those who are unhappy. Happy people cope better with life's challenges than unhappy people do. It should be obvious to us, even without the studies, that happy people make better life partners, parents, children, friends, employers and employees.

To anyone who wants to find a spouse and get married or find a new job, the most important way to begin is to start enjoying your life more now. Nobody wants to be around, or introduce to their friend or even hire a sourpuss! Just think of the people you like to be around. Your favorite people are the ones who genuinely appreciate life. There is no one that you will spend more time with than yourself, so you may as well begin upping the happiness quotient in your own life.

When my son was a teenager, he applied to go to a prestigious yeshiva or high school of intense Jewish studies. I accompanied him as he went for his entrance exam and interview. After my son met with the head rabbi of the school, I went into the rabbi's office.

The rabbi remarked, "Your son likes himself very much." I agreed cautiously because I didn't know where he was taking this. Then the rabbi continued, "That is good. If he doesn't like himself, he can't like me." (Whew!)

This is a very true dynamic. It is also why the verse in the Torah reads, "Love your neighbor as yourself." First, a person has to love themselves, and then they can love their neighbor.

The same is true with happiness. If I cannot be happy with myself, I won't be satisfied with anyone else.

There are those unfortunate souls who believe that happiness is earned and they somehow don't deserve it. They are sorely mistaken. Would you ever tell your child that he doesn't deserve to be happy? Sure, you might discipline him in order that he understands consequences. Teaching accountability and morality is just that—teaching. One of the most painful emotions a parent can feel is that their child is unhappy.

The reason we need to get married and have children is that these relationships serve as a paradigm for our relationship with G-d. This paradigm gives us tremendous insight and wisdom for living. As painful as it is for us to have miserable children (that is, how painful, so to speak), it is for G-d when we are miserable. Everything that we want to accomplish in life can be accomplished more effectively if we are feeling good about who and what we are.

Happiness is an obligation to G-d

Why does G-d care if I'm happy or not?

Ask yourself this question, "What is the one thing I want/wish for my children?" Most people answer, "I want only the best for them." That is what the Almighty wants for us.

Again, our primary relationship with G-d is best compared to a loving father. In the same way that we are happy when our children are happy and sad when they are troubled, it is the same with G-d. He is happy or sad (so to speak) depending on the state of His children. The Bible states the divine obligation to be happy in black and white when we are told in Deuteronomy 26:11, "You shall rejoice with all the good that the Almighty has given you." This is a commandment to be happy and appreciate the good that G-d bestows on us.

Does G-d need us to be happy?

Abraham publicized the concept of monotheism. Eventually the Jewish people accepted upon themselves the responsibility to be a "light upon the nations", and spread this concept. Monotheism doesn't just mean that there is only one G-d, but that G-d is one. G-d is infinite. He is omnipotent, omnipresent, and omniscient. There is no way to add or subtract from G-d. Infinity plus or minus a million is still infinity. A perfect G-d has no needs, lacks, or wants. If He did, He would not be perfect.

Being that, G-d has no needs or true desires, when a person feels they need to "do something" for G-d, it may seem to be a noble thought; but in essence, it is attributing a very humanistic aspect to the Almighty.

The truth is that in order to have a relationship with G-d, we need to anthropomorphize him. We must personify G-d in a way that allows us to carry on conversations, laugh, and cry with Him and depend on Him.

If there is nothing that G-d needs from us, why does He command us to do so many things in the Bible?

The commandments are not for G-d, they are for us. The Kabbala teaches that each one of the commandments is a principle for attaining pleasure in our lives. The deeper we understand the essence of the commandment, the more benefit we will have.

How we instruct our children is a fantastic illustration of this point.

When you give your children ice cream, you demand that they say please and thank-you. (If you don't, you should!) Not because you need them to say thank-you, but because *they* need to say please and thank-you. It is good for them to express appreciation when someone is good to them. If they do, they will grow and understand that others have helped them, and in turn, they should help others. If they don't, they will grow up to be ungrateful, selfish animals.

We command our children to do many things: clean up their room, brush their teeth, and do their homework. All these things are ultimately for *their* good.

When they are younger, they rarely appreciate the value of personal hygiene and your other commandments. However, as children grow and mature, they will realize the value of your instructions. Eventually, they will appreciate that it was really beneficial for them to do all of these things, and they will probably command their children to do the same.

This same concept applies to our relationship with the Almighty. Every time we fulfill a commandment, it is not G-d who benefits; it is us who benefit!

The Jewish religion contains a prayer that one should say after eating. The source for this is also in the Bible when we are told, "You shall eat, be satisfied, and bless the Lord your G-d." There are many people who eat a lot from this world and are never satisfied. There are some who don't take much from this world and are still very satisfied. However, we are commanded to partake from this world, be satiated, and recognize that our gifts are from the Almighty.

Imagine, the Almighty, Creator of the universe, commands you to partake from this world and *enjoy it!*

Many people have difficulty with the Bible because they don't want a G-d, with whom they have little or no connection with, telling and obligating them as to what is right and wrong. They feel that G-d should not play a role in their reward or punishment. Perhaps these people would be more open to seeing the truth of the Bible if they understood that the Almighty wants them to be happy. This is so important to G-d, that the Bible even teaches that the reason for all retribution and aggravation in life, is that people do not serve G-d with joy in their hearts (Deuteronomy 28:47).

Can you really obligate someone to feel something?

One time when explaining this concept to a group of people, a woman jumped up and objected, "Happiness is an emotion, you can't obligate somebody to feel emotions!" I asked her if she had children and if they ever fought. She replied that she had three boys who sometimes fought like animals. "Do they ever say 'I hate my brother'?" I asked. "Of course," she said. "And what do you say?" I continued, "You have to *love* your brother?"

As parents, we often *wish* to command emotions. What we really do though is command actions that lead to emotions. It basically goes like this, "Love your brother! You can't? Even if you don't like your brother, don't hit him. And share your toy! And by the way, put a smile on your face!"

Being happy is actually a natural state of being

One of the most beautiful aspects of young children is that as long as they have what they need, they are happy. When you see a cranky kid, you ask, "What is wrong?" Maybe they are cold, hungry, tired, or being teased by an older sibling. The assumption is that something *must* be wrong. Why? Because the natural state of humanity is to be happy.

When we grow up, we learn to be unhappy even if most of our needs are being met.

I was nineteen years old and going to school, living in Jerusalem. Most of the people who went to this *yeshiva* (a school of advanced Judaic studies where people are often trained to become rabbis) had already received a university degree and were between five to ten years older than me. Sometimes my thoughts would drift to the fraternity parties that I was missing, and my fellow students were very serious about their rabbinical studies. I went to my rabbi with the concern that because I was so much younger than everyone, maybe I was being forced to grow up too fast.

He said the most amazing thing to me.

"Yitz, most people, when they say they are growing up, they mean they are giving up. Growing up actually means taking responsibility. You can never grow up too fast."

When we are young, we are more altruistic and dreamy about our future. As people grow, they often become more realistic about their plight in life. The pressures of daily life increase, and it just becomes more difficult to connect with our naturally happy selves.

What if I really don't feel happy?

If you cannot bring yourself to feel the emotion of being happy, you at least need to act as if you are happy. There are two benefits to this. The first is that we have a Talmudic principle, that we have already mentioned, that says "a man is emotionally pulled after his actions." In other words, if you act happy, you will become happy. The way we do this is by engaging in certain actions and behaviors that engender feelings of joy within us. Yes, it is true. "Fake it, fake it, fake it until you make it" is a Talmudic principle.

The second reason to act happy even if you are not is that people will respond to you in a totally different way if you radiate joy. When this happens, various windows of opportunities will seem to magically open up to you and give you real reasons to rejoice. If the reason for punishment in the Bible is because His people did not serve G-d with joy, then it stands to reason that there will be great rewards for people who walk this earth with great joy in their hearts.

The Talmud explains that anyone who rejoices in their afflictions will bring salvation to the world. "Salvation to the world" is the ultimate prize. It refers to the coming of the messiah and the perfection of humanity.

In "Secret # 4: Focusing on the Good," we will learn strategies on how to deal with troubles. For now, recognize that because it is so difficult to be happy during bad times, if we are able to stay focused on being happy, or at least acting like we are happy, the rewards are incredibly valuable.

Clay Digger Story: A tale on "Staying Happy Pays!"

Once there was a poor man who used to make his living by digging clay and selling it.

One day, he was digging in the mud when suddenly he found a jewel that looked like it must have been worth a fortune! The clay digger had no idea how much it was worth, so he went to a jeweler to have it appraised.

The jeweler told him it was so valuable there was no one in their country with enough money to buy it! In order to sell such a jewel, the clay digger would have to travel to London. But being poor, the man did not have the money to make the journey. He went and sold everything he had and went from house to house asking for contributions until he had sufficient money to get to the port where he could travel by sea to London.

He wanted to board the ship, but he did not have enough money for the fare. He went to the captain and showed him the precious stone. The captain immediately took him aboard the ship with great enthusiasm, saying, "I know that you are good for the fare, but just in case you get something foolish in your head, you better not try and cheat me or I will rip your head off!" The captain gave him a special first-class cabin with every luxury befitting person of very high rank.

The clay digger's cabin had a window overlooking the sea. He would sit there enjoying himself immensely, rejoicing over the diamond, especially at mealtimes when it was easy to reflect on his good fortune.

One day, he sat down to eat and placed the diamond on the table, right in front of him so that he could enjoy it. After his meal, he took a nap. While asleep, the cabin boy came in to clean up and took the tablecloth with all the crumbs and, without even noticing the diamond, shook everything into the sea!

When the clay digger awoke, he realized what had happened. He almost went out of his mind with worry and anguish. What was he to do? The captain was a pirate who would murder him for the boat fare.

Still, the clay digger *pretended* to be happy—as if he was unaware that anything had happened to his precious gem.

Everyday during the voyage, the captain would talk to the clay digger for several hours. The clay digger made such a show of being happy that the captain didn't notice anything unusual.

The captain said to him, "I know you are clever and honest. I have a large quantity of grain with me in the boat to sell in London—I can make a big profit. My fear is that I will be accused of embezzling from the royal treasury. Let the transaction be made in *your* name, and I will reward you handsomely." The clay digger felt it was a good idea, and he agreed.

As soon as they arrived in London, the captain died, and everything was left in the hands of the clay digger! The cargo was in fact worth many times more than the diamond was!

A great rabbi who lived in nineteenth century, Rabbi Nachman from Breslov, interpreted this story in the following way. The truth is that the diamond did not belong to the clay digger—and the proof is that he lost it. The grain was destined to belong to him—and the proof is that he kept it. And the clay digger only acquired what was his because he forced himself to stay happy.

Can just wanting to be happy make you happy?

No. The world is filled with examples of people who accomplished great things primarily on the basis of their dedication and commitment. Every motivational speaker has his or her favorite story of the against-all-odds hero.

And it is true that when we really want something, G-d creates angels, spiritual forces, to guide and help us along that path. "G-d helps those who help themselves" is an accurate description of this concept. However, many of our most basic accomplishments are dependent on things outside of our control.

"Where there's a will, there's a way!" is not always true. I might desperately 'will' to be an NBA superstar, but I'm only five feet eight inches and not *that* coordinated. The amount of money a person makes and whether or not your child gets good grades in school or drives across town safely, depends on outside influences. The economy, teachers, and other safety-conscious drivers will affect the outcome of these events.

These are all things that involve the will and participation of other people or natural physical abilities. There are things we can do that we consider making the required reasonable effort. Working hard, networking with the right people, and doing homework are all important. At the same time, because there are so many factors outside of our control, doing these things may not ensure success.

What we *can* do is put forth a strong effort in making living joyfully our driving force. This combined with the following five secrets will guarantee a happier you!

Points to remember:

- If we want to live joyfully, we *will* live joyfully.
- Happiness is your choice and a product of your decision to be happier.
- More than a decision, living joyfully is an obligation to ourselves, to others, and to G-d.
- Even if you don't truly feel happy on the inside, behave as if you are happy on the outside and you will be blessed!

Your Notes

Secret # 3

Seeing Is Being:

Expanding Your Reality

The Rodger Bannister story

ROGER BANNISTER WAS a physician by profession who competed in track-and-field in the 1950s. He taught the world one of the most important lessons in personal growth. Up until that point, most people thought it was physically impossible for anyone to run a mile distance in less than four minutes. On May 6, 1954, Roger Bannister broke the four-minute mile. Dr. Bannister's historic world-record time lasted only forty-six days. Within a very short time, sixteen other runners eclipsed his world-record mark. When asked why he thought so many people broke the record so quickly after he did, Bannister cited a "collective mental limitation." In other words, once he broke the record, it became conceivable for others to do a four-minute-mile run. Once people really thought it was achievable, they started doing it!

The first step in creating a different reality is envisioning a different reality. Actually seeing yourself doing whatever you want to be doing. What would you look like if you were living 15 percent more joyfully than you do now? What would your life look like? What kind of blessings would you now be open to? If we really want to live more joyfully, then we have to see ourselves living more joyfully. When you look into the mirror, smile. The person looking at you always smiles back! As you plan out your day, see yourself experiencing happiness, no matter how things are panning out.

I think therefore I am, I see therefore I be.

The concept of positive visualization doesn't just apply to being happy; it applies to every area of life. If you want to have a better marriage, you have to be able to see yourself being part of a fulfilling relationship. If you want to have greater wealth, you have to envision yourself capable of achieving it.

Imagine for a moment the difference between James and Charlie. James has a very cold relationship with his wife. On his way home from work, before he walks in the door at the end of the day, he anticipates his wife badgering him with questions, criticizing his decisions, and demanding that he help more with the children. He is tired, hungry and really wants nothing to do with anybody. When he sees her car in the driveway, James tightens up, knowing that he is in for an unpleasant interaction. Going home is the most stressful part of his day.

Charlie used to have a similar experience until he came to speak with me. I advised him that on the way home he should pull the car over in a safe place and rest for fifteen minutes. Keep a snack in the car and eat something right before he arrives. (Few things are more irritable than a man who is famished!) I told him to take two minutes before he walks into the door and reflect on how fortunate he is to be married to his wife and have their children. I told him to put a smile on his face and anticipate the pleasure of giving his family the first half hour of him being home.

At first, it was a disaster! The assault and berating from his wife continued. However, slowly it began to change. He was in a better mood walking in, so he didn't yell back or retreat to his man cave. Everyone picked up on his change of behavior, and they changed too. Now, instead of staying later at work many times every week, which only exasperated the problem, Charlie now looks forward to going home and being with his family.

Amazing, it only took a few minor adjustments, including visualizing how he wanted it to be, and being at home became a pleasurable experience.

What is the difference between visualizing and fantasizing?

Roger Bannister's accomplishment was a product of his vision, not because he achieved it, but because the four-minute mile was the result of his own efforts. He had a training regimen and took action to achieve his goal. This is in contrast to someone who hopes that an outside force would make his vision a reality.

One of the very few things in life that we can control is our vision, our perception of reality. When we rely on others to accomplish things that are important for us, we often are sorely disappointed. Therefore, it is crucial to distinguish between those things that are in our control and those that aren't. Setting a goal that it is not directly dependent on our efforts to achieve is not a good idea. It is a fantasy. What ends up happening is people start sitting around, thinking how great it would be to have this accomplishment under their belts, drinking another cup of coffee, waiting, thinking, drinking more coffee, checking another e-mail. Not only is this an exercise in futility but a person's self-esteem takes a beating as well, because they don't end up accomplishing what they desire.

If there are practical steps that you can take to touch your dream, then you must establish a pathway and set forth the appropriate effort. This will turn the dream into reality.

Jason tells me often that he wants to get married and have a family. The problem is that he spends nights and weekends alone in his apartment and makes little effort to meet other singles. He doesn't even remind his family and married friends that he is looking for someone. Even though I firmly believe that everyone has a soul mate and there is a top for every pot, Jason's dream of marriage is in reality, for now, a fantasy.

If you want to experience this more:

- Visualize yourself living a main goal of your life for two minutes straight.
- Identify what specific courses of action you would need to take in order to actualize the vision.
- Find a role model or coach who can give you guidance on which steps you can take.

According to the effort is the reward.

—*The Talmud*

Bannister did not drop his time by thirty seconds overnight. It took years of training, discipline, and sweat to slowly inch himself into a world-class athlete and then champion.

If Jason really wants to get married, he will have to seek out appropriate social events, community activities, and engage others in his search for a wife. But that's not all! For most singles, if they really want to get married, they probably need to embark on a program of self-improvement to make themselves more desirable. They should identify the kind of person that they want and then ask themselves, "Why would that kind of person want me?" The answers to these questions will guide them in their self-improvement program. I always advise that they should pray for divine help as well. If you wish to live a more joyful life, then you must be willing to pay the price in effort in order to reap the rewards.

Don't be intimidated by the mountain!

A friend of mine called me with excitement in his voice; an incredibly wealthy man, Sam, just invited him to a private meeting with Tom, one of the most influential Jewish thinkers of our time. Sam has a very large charitable foundation and realized that he did not want his money to go fund the opera or a museum, but rather, he wanted to help the Jewish people. The purpose of the meeting was to ask Tom for suggestions on how to best use his foundation.

My friend asked me, "If I get a chance to give an opinion, what do you think I should say?"

I told him that Sam should take his foundation and fund a cadre of charismatic, knowledgeable rabbis. He should put them on television and radio to spread the universal messages within Jewish Values to as wide an audience as possible. In this way, the foundation's funds will accomplish two things: 1) Reaching the largest audience of Jews who are disconnected from their spiritual heritage , and 2) Strengthen the bonds of mutual understanding and respect among the community of mankind.

I continued to explain to him that I thought there was only one issue to deal with now, the assimilation of Jews away from Jewish values. What the Nazis couldn't do to us seventy years ago, we are doing to ourselves through ignorance and assimilation. We are supposed to be a light unto the nations, and with so many Jews so far away from their heritage, we simply are not bringing enough goodness into the world the way we should.

My friend called me after the meeting to update me on how it went. He said that they spent most of the meeting talking about developing a positive PR campaign for Israel. What happened when my friend brought up the issue of addressing the assimilation of Jewish people away from Jewish values?

Sam and Tom both agreed that it is the most important issue to deal with, but they didn't want to address it. Why? Because it was too big!

My friend and I were both astounded. How could it be that these two giants in the Jewish world were intimidated by the problem?

They could visualize making millions of dollars and selling millions of books, but they could not visualize changing millions of lives.

Don't Be Afraid of a Big Goal!

When Michael Jordan was giving a speech after being inducted into the Basketball Hall of Fame, he indicated that one day he might still be playing basketball when he is fifty years old. In response to the laughter of the audience, he said, "Oh, don't laugh. Never say never because limits, like fears, are often just illusions."

One of the reasons people are hesitant to create a vision and goal of a better life is they don't want to fail. If I don't dream or think of something grand, then I won't fail. If I don't tell anyone about any aspirations, then when they don't manifest themselves, no one will think that I'm a loser.

"You don't score on 100% of the shots you never take"

—Wayne Gretzky.

The wise man is not discouraged by big challenges; he finds a way!

There is a Jewish legend about a king who banished two prisoners to the outskirts of the kingdom and commanded them to move a mountain of sand into the ocean. Only then would they be released from their punishment.

The foolish man took his shovel and dug for a while until he gave up and became resigned to the fact that he will spend the rest of his life banished away from his family.

The wise man started digging and digging. When he noticed that a crevasse began to develop in the sand, he dug a little more in the right place until the whole mountain of sand flowed by itself to the sea.

One of the sages of the Talmud, Rabbi Tarfon, used to exhort to his students that they are not required to complete the task yet they are not free to withdraw from it either. So often in life the mountain towers above us and it just seems too big to conquer. If we remember his teaching, we can approach the challenge with a feeling of confidence that whatever we accomplish, it is worthwhile.

When you want to be inspired to conquer a mountain—just look at another mountain!

I recently took one of my sons to Whistler, British Columbia, one of the premier ski resorts in the world. As we stood at the peak of one of the snow covered mountains, preparing to launch ourselves down the ski run, I couldn't help but be awestruck by the beauty of the Canadian Rockies. The unhampered view of the snow covered mountains stretching as far as the eye could see was nothing short of breathtaking. From the very bottom of my soul, I spontaneously blurted out, "G-d, if you can create these, then you can fix every problem in my life!"

Jewish wisdom teaches us that if G-d wanted, He could have created the whole universe without color, just black and white with shades of grey. The structure of biology could have been made simple instead of complex. The natural world could have been made without variation or conflict, instead it was created with disparate forces and elements. Fortunately for us, the Almighty wanted mankind to be inspired by His creation. For that reason, among others, we are obligated to study a certain amount of biology and earth sciences. This is so we will understand and be inspired by all facets of the magnificent world G-d created for us. The result of attuning our 'eye' to see the world's most spectacular sights, whether they are achievements of G-d or of humanity, is that our spirits are lifted, our dreams and aspirations are encouraged, and we begin to realize that there is no limit as to what we may accomplish.

In a similar vein, when we notice and examine the world's greatness; great monuments, thoughts, inventions or deeds that excite and inspire us, we learn that most of them were, at one time, considered to have been "impossible". What a revelation it is to realize that most of mankind's greatest accomplishments came into existence by perseverance and courage! And, coming full circle back to ourselves, the fortitude and determination of others can boost our own supply of these qualities, just when we need that little extra burst of courage and grit.

Remember the last time you were at an amusement park and your children were goading you to go with them on one of those enormous, terrifying roller coasters? Did you summon the strength not to 'chicken out' or embarrass yourself? And, if you did, how did you summon the courage to step into that coaster? Perhaps you did what I do; watch all of the people getting off the ride and say to yourself, "If they survived, then I will too."

"Every journey begins with a single step"

As the saying goes, "How does one eat an elephant? One bite at a time."

A worm can start to gnaw away at a tree, drying out just a little bit of its trunk. Slowly, as more and more of the tree dries out, it begins to rot and, eventually, falls down. It is amazing how such a small worm can topple such a big tree!

I have found one of the best strategies to deal with problems or accomplish large tasks is to break them down into smaller parts. I might not be able to handle a big problem, but if I break it into one hundred sections, I can handle one of those pieces rather quickly. Then my whole problem is a little smaller.

No Free lunches!

Milton Friedman, a Nobel laureate economist, was once asked to summarize all economics in one sentence. He responded, "There are no free lunches!" These are wise words to live by, not just in economics but in every aspect of life. I Admire M. Friedman

Whether your motto is "You get out what you put in"; "No pain, no gain"; or the Talmudic version, "According to the effort is the reward," they all send a similar message. In life, there is a price to pay for everything. We pay for every action we take. As a matter of fact, if you think there is something you do that does not exact a price, then you haven't thought it through! From life changing issues like who to marry or how many children to have, to the mundane issues like taking time to shower and brush our teeth, everything has a cost. What ever we are doing at any given moment, we could be doing something else, and there is a consequence as a result of our choice. There will be a cost involved in acquiring an education; there will be a cost in not acquiring an education. There are very real benefits and prices to pay for remaining single and there are benefits and prices to pay for getting married. The same paradigm exists in every area of life.

Once a person is at peace with this reality, when it comes time to make a payment on something they value, they won't be shocked. One of the reasons many people have difficulty in their marriages or in the work place is because they are not prepared to put in the effort that is necessary to succeed. When I walk into a store to buy something, I am emotionally prepared to reach into my wallet and pay for it. People who accept that they must pay a price for their decisions, not only accomplish great things, but are more likely to have a fantastic time while doing it.

How much are you charging me for that again?

After you make peace with the fact that everything in life has a price, the next step is to figure out how much something will cost. The cost might come in the form a commitment or investment of your of time, emotional effort, or money. The benefit we are seeking might require that we forgo legitimate pleasures for awhile or maybe for forever! To have a good marriage, raise children, develop a successful career—all have enormous costs. The benefits are also tremendous and, most of the time, worth it.

Many people in business become familiar with the following calculation. Before pursuing a client, they ask themselves three questions. 1) How much time and effort will it take me to secure the client and do the job? 2) How much money could I make from it? 3) Is the money worth my time and effort?

If the client is a nice, well connected, honest individual; you might even do the job for a lot less money. If the client is a pain in the neck and he doesn't pay his bills promptly; if you take the job at all, you might try and charge more.

This calculation is applicable to almost every area of life and is essential to experiencing true happiness.

If I know the cost of something, I can decide to pay it or not. Whichever path I choose to go in, the future is now in my hands and I can claim responsibility for my decisions. ONLY when I have explored and weighed the potential benefits with the potential costs of something, can I fully 'own' my decisions. If I'm uncomfortable having to pay for something or I feel like I am overpaying, then it is up to me to keep paying or not. This forces me to constantly evaluate the benefit of my situation. When I appreciate the benefit, even if the cost is heavy, I can be joyful because it is worth the price.

Sometimes, the benefits are not worth the price. What should you do? Stop paying and forgo the benefit. If you are sitting at the theater watching a lousy movie, why pay for the price of admission *and* not enjoy the next hour and a half of your life? Get up and leave!

When weighing the benefits and costs of more serious issues, like your marriage, you should seek a second opinion to help evaluate the consequences better. The cost to your children and career, aside from alimony, might be more expensive than you originally thought, so proceed with caution.

The Pleasure-Pain Principle

Ask most people what the opposite of pain is and they will say pleasure. That is not correct. The opposite of pain is no pain or comfort. This is perhaps the most significant confusion in the Western world today. The result of confusing comfort with pleasure is that we have become a very decadent society.

I don't deny that lying on a beach with a gentle breeze cooling the sun's warmth, listening to the waves come in with a cold piña colada in your hand is very enjoyable and at times it can be very beneficial. However, it is a huge mistake for a person to make this relaxing experience one of their major life's goals. Ultimately, it will cause them to miss out on many greater pleasures and possibly lead to great misery.

Vince Lombardi inspired championships by saying, "No pain, no gain!"

People appreciate what they work for most. The Talmudic version of Coach Lombardi's motto "According to the effort is the reward," is not just a statement of reality, it is sound advice for living.

What about a good bargain?

Sometimes a person finds him/herself involved in looking for "something for nothing." This attitude is not only an exercise in futility but extremely counterproductive to personal happiness. The reason is because "something for nothing" doesn't exist! If it is too good to be true, it isn't true.

When a person's life's ambition is to receive as much as they can for as little as possible, it leads to some very destructive perceptions and emotions. If they *ARE* successful at sucking out a lot of "whatever" from society, they develop an attitude of entitlement, which will retard their ability to be happy. If they *ARE NOT* successful, then they will live in frustration, always desiring what they aren't getting.

Entitlements

Putting forth the effort and paying for our pleasures is not a contradiction to appreciating what we have; it is a prerequisite. We appreciate specifically those things we pay for. When we pay for things, we attach value to them. Often, the more we pay the more value we attach. When we attach value, we appreciate; when we appreciate, we enjoy.

> **If you want to experience this more:**
>
> - Identify for yourself three pleasures that you would really like to enjoy/experience.
> - Evaluate the cost and benefit of each pleasure in time, effort, and money (or any other area of expense).
> - Decide if the pleasure is worth the cost, and then pursue it; or if the pleasure is not worth the cost, feel good about not pursuing it.

The Ability to live joyfully is very doable!

Another piece of life wisdom that every parent knows is, you don't demand the impossible from your children. It is fruitless at best and destructive at worst. One of the best ways to create a person with poor no self-worth is to consistently require them to do things out of their reach. This way, their life is a series of one failure after another.

Don't get me wrong; I am a big believer in the philosophy of life that says, "If you shoot for the stars, then at least you will get to the moon!" Many of my sermons and seminars encourage and inspire others to be more than they can be and to dream higher than they ever thought possible. However, when it comes to parenting, business, and G-dly commands, the goals must be achievable. If not, they will over time, become meaningless, empty and worst of all, even abandoned.

For this reason, you need to know that living joyfully is within your capabilities. We are supposed live with the reality that life is good, I mean GREAT!

We are going to find that the ability to live joyfully is a spiritual accomplishment and resides completely within us.

"There is no place like home"

There is an old Jewish tale about a poor peasant from a small town in Poland. Every night he dreams about a treasure chest buried under a bridge in Prague. Unable to escape the dream, the peasant takes it as a sign from G-d that he should travel to find his riches. When he gets to the bridge, he sees that it is being guarded carefully by members of the royal army. Carefully, the peasant sneaks in the middle of the night to excavate the treasure from beneath the bridge. When he is caught by a guard, he has no choice but to reveal his dream. The officer scoffs at the man, calling him foolish, saying, "I also dream every night that there is treasure buried under the brick oven of some poor Polish peasant, but you don't see me traveling across Europe chasing my dreams!"

The peasant returns home immediately. What is the first thing he does? He digs under his own oven. And lo and behold, he finds a box of treasure!

Why did the peasant have to travel to Prague to get the message? G-d could have given him the dream that the riches were under his own oven. The peasant needed to have faith in his dreams and exert effort to accomplish his goal.

Why were the riches found in the peasant's own home? The peasant had to realize that you don't have to go very far to find the greatest treasures in your life.

We also need confidence in our goal of living joyfully and understand that even though it will probably take some work, the springs of happiness are buried within us and are ready to burst out.

Happiness set point

For years, researches in the field of positive psychology have discussed something called the happiness set-point theory. There is conflicting research on whether or not the theory is true. A recent Google search on the topic found over 7 million results discussing its validity. However for practical purposes, one can be empowered to live a happier life whether it is true or not.

The theory basically states that just as people have a genetically designed weight set point, we also have an emotional happiness set point.

I have a weight set point of about 150 lb. (Okay, 155 lb.!) Unless I exercise or diet with conviction, my weight will naturally gravitate around that 155 lb. range.

A similar dynamic occurs with happiness. Some people are naturally predisposed to being upbeat and happy; others are predisposed to being a little sad and melancholy. That is because of their happiness set point. Researches say that the happiness set point accounts for about 50-60 percent of a person's emotional state. This can explain why wonderful events like winning the lottery or having a baby will only cause a temporary lift in a person's emotions. Tragic events like losing one's home to disaster or even a death in the family will provide also only temporary depressions from one's natural state of happiness.

The few exceptions to this rule will include: losing a limb, perpetual unemployment, and a death of a spouse whom one has been married to for most of their life. These events are so traumatic that either one never recovers totally from them or, according to some researchers; one actually changes their set point.

Good news, bad news, and really good news

First, the good news. Every one of us has a certain innately genetically programmed amount "aptitude for happiness." Even if it is less than you would like, everyone has the ability to feel up, positive, peppy, and joyful at times. Happiness is something as natural to the human being as growing up. As a matter of fact, if you look at a baby, when they aren't distracted by hunger, tiredness, or the discomfort of a soiled diaper, they are happy.

The bad news is that we all have a predisposition, a limit as it were, to an inherent range of happiness. Some people out there that will have to work very hard to be in a good mood even if there is nothing really wrong with their lives. They won't even know why they are down; they are just down. Their genetic makeup is such that they are almost stuck at a particular level of joy.

Then again, the *really* good news is: at least 40-50 percent of your emotional makeup is up to you, and up to you only! So even if you were one of the unfortunate souls to have a severe challenge in living joyfully, having 40 percent of your emotional makeup left up to your choice leaves a lot of room for improvement.

As a matter of fact, I think that most people would be thrilled if they could increase their personal joy by 10 or 15 percent. That amount is purely a consequence of our wisdom, motivation, and commitment to accomplish joyful living.

Points to remember:

- Roger Bannister story—first, you have to visualize yourself doing it!
- A proper vision is one that is directly affected by your efforts.
- According to the *effort* is the reward.
- The wise man is not discouraged by big challenges; he finds a way!
- Living with joy is no dream . . . it is very doable!

Your Notes

Sitting in my garden with a Book & my dog, I Feel Happy

Secret # 4

Focusing on the Good:

Training Your Mind's Eye

WHAT IS THE most important concept a parent can impress upon their children?

To know that life is good.

Once a person is real with how marvelous it is to be alive, no challenge is insurmountable.

In a very real sense, even though life is filled with its ups and downs, trials and tribulations, almost everyone would agree that being alive beats the alternative. When one is not distracted with their troubles and obligations, they see clearly the beauty and goodness of this world. When one is free from problems, it is easy and natural to be happy.

As we have said before, we evaluate every situation in one of three ways; positive, negative, or neutral.

Training our eyes to see the positive, the beauty of every situation, is just that—training.

The Talmud terms this "a good eye" and it is considered one of the most praiseworthy character traits a person can develop.

The story is told of a great second-century sage called Rabbi Yochanan. Once, he was walking in the countryside with some students, and they came upon the rotting carcass of a dog. The students recoiled and remarked about the awful stench emanating from the carcass. Rabbi Yochanan said, "Yes, but look how white the dog's teeth are!" One of the traits that made Rabbi Yochanan so great, was his ability to focus on the positive of every situation.

There would be times when my kids would come home from school complaining about their teachers. I would say to them, "Fine, I want to hear about all the problems, but first tell me three good things that happened to you in school today." This little exercise would always put overwhelming troubles into perspective.

Everything is for the good

The Talmud relates a story of one of the most influential rabbis of all time named Rabbi Akiva, who lived in Israel during the second century.

One time before he was well-known, Rabbi Akiva was traveling, and he needed a place to spend the night. He knocked on the door of one of the homes in the town he had stopped in but was refused hospitality. He was not upset, for he realized, "Everything G-d does is for the good."

Rabbi Akiva tried another home and again he was not offered hospitality and again his reaction remained the same, "Everything G-d does is for the good." Even after he had gone from door to door, realizing that no one in the town was going to accept him as a guest, he still said, "Everything G-d does is for the good."

Rabbi Akiva had no choice but to camp in a forest on the outskirts of town. He was traveling with a donkey to carry his packages, a rooster to wake him up early each morning, and a lamp with which he could study at night. Shortly after he encamped, a lion devoured his donkey; his rooster was killed by another predator; and if that wasn't bad enough, a strong wind blew out his fire. After each of these events, Rabbi Akiva told himself again and again, "Everything G-d does is for the good."

The following morning, he discovered that during the night, a Roman legion had attacked this village and taken its people as captives. Had he been accepted as a guest in one of these homes, he too would have been taken captive.

If his donkey or rooster had been alive, their braying and crowing probably would have attracted the legionnaires' attention. Had his candle remained burning, they would have been able to see him in the forest. Everything that happened was for the good.

According to Jewish thought, this is not just having a positive mental attitude; this is reality.

If a person believes in an all-powerful, infinite G-d who loves them more than they love their children, then it makes sense that even if there are major challenges in one's life, everything that happens is for the good.

Rabbi Akiva's approach to life leads a person to appreciate that even though a situation may be painful or unpleasant, it will somehow lead to a positive outcome.

There are certainly situations that are essentially impossible for the "sufferers" to identify any good; for example, being the mother of a child who was killed by a drunk driver.

However, when we develop our life attitudes, we use generalizations. Generally speaking, if we were to know the positive results of a painful event from the outset, we would decide that it is worth enduring most negative experiences for the sake of the positive benefit.

Rabbi Akiva taught that even when a person does not have such foreknowledge, he should have the faith that G-d is involved in his experience and should accept everything with happiness and joy.

Why is there so much suffering in the world?

The Bible tells how one time Moses, the greatest prophet who ever lived or will ever live, asked G-d to show him his "face." G-d's response is, "No man can see my face and live."

Judaism has always rejected the concept that G-d has any physical body, so clearly in this context, Moses is not requesting a physical peek at the Lord. The Talmud explains that what Moses was really asking was, "Why do bad things happen to good people?" G-d's response is, "No man can see my face and live."

In other words, there are certain things that we simply cannot understand while living in this world. We are finite and limited; G-d is infinite and therefore unlimited. Our tradition teaches that when we die, our soul ascends to "the world of truth" where all will be revealed. Until then, our test is to strive to whenever possible, see the good in even the most painful, tragic events.

It is very positive that we are bothered by suffering. You probably wouldn't want a relationship with anyone who was so callous to another person's less fortunate plight. Insensitivity severely retards one's ability to have a relationship with others or G-d. Also, the selfishness that is bred by insensitivity will ultimately hamper that person's ability to have a truly joyful life.

Be that as it may, it is wise to empathize and do what we can to alleviate others' pain but not to allow our lives to be consumed by tragic events that occur in our world every day.

Life is a series of struggles

If you are playing basketball and the other team is running you ragged, you can call a time out and regain your composure. Life doesn't work that way, there are no "time outs." Every person encounters many struggles and challenges every day of his or her life. As soon as you think you have conquered one challenge, it seems the next one is waiting for you just around the corner.

Being at peace with this reality is crucial for living a happy life. Otherwise you might spend your whole life looking for a world without pain, suffering or frustration; a world that does not exist. That can lead to a very disappointing existence. On the other hand, once we recognize that every day will contain new challenges, we can learn to accept them and find ways that they can actually enhance our days.

Even though everyone's challenges are different, the one thing that we all have in common is that we must deal with them every day. People have daily struggles with their health, finances, relationships, food, fidelity, arrogance and even depression. The list of how many difficulties exist in our personal lives is limited only by the number of people on the planet.

This is what the Torah alludes to in the story of Cain and Able. Before Cain kills his brother, they both bring an offering to G-d. Abel offers up the very best of his sheep, which the Almighty accepts. But, when Cain offers up less than the very best of his crop, G-d rejects his substandard 'gift.' Cain responds to G-d's rejection by becoming ever more annoyed, angry and depressed. Observing the increasingly petulant Cain, G-d asks him "Why are you annoyed, and why have you become depressed? Surely, if you improve yourself, you will be forgiven." The Almighty gives Cain the freedom to choose his own next move when he says, "If you do not improve yourself, sin rests at your door. Its desire is toward you, but you can conquer it." (Genesis 4:6-7)

At this point, what is Cain's actual sin?

He became depressed.

Why did he become depressed?

He felt rejected by G-d.

How did G-d respond to Cain's depressed attitude?

G-d told Cain to work on himself so that he would be forgiven and not have to feel rejected.

What did G-d say would happen if Cain chose *not* to improve himself?

G-d told Cain that the opportunity to sin would always be available and appealing, but that if Cain chose to turn away from his inclination to do wrong, he would beat sin—hands down!

In other words, we live in a world where there are, and always will be, multitudes of opportunities to become annoyed and depressed. However, if we are aware that our struggles provide opportunities for us to improve ourselves, we can conquer rather than succumbing to the things that challenge us.

I often encounter people who tell me they just want to make enough money so that they don't have to worry about their finances; they just want to live without stress. That sounds nice. Who wouldn't want to live that way? Well, I'm sorry to be the bearer of bad news, but it just isn't going to happen. Even if things would work out so that they don't have to worry about money any more, new or different problems will arise. And, I've seen it happen all too often, that when people do overcome what they thought was the only stumbling block between them and a stress-free life of bliss, the next problem they encounter is far worse and more stressful than their original issue. A high ranking executive with a multi billion dollar corporation said on many occasions, "Be careful what you wish for. You just might get it."

Over the years I have had the incredible opportunity to travel abroad to Israel and other countries. Whereas every trip was enriching, and pleasurable, I don't recall one of these wonderful trips that were stress-free. From last minute shopping for things I would need on the trip, getting to the airport on time, making arrangements for travel and lodging and then reacting to inevitable changes to our arrangements, to meeting up with people in foreign cities where none of us had been before, there are numerous aspects of every trip that are stressful. And, believe it or not, these are the moments in life that are supposed to be fun!

The only time we are not confronted with stress and struggles is after we are dead, when the game is over. Those who try to run away from their struggles often do not live peaceful lives but rather end up digging themselves deeper into their own difficulties. The more at peace we become with this reality the easier it will be to accept our challenges and face them head-on, with energy, determination and, after some practice, with enthusiasm.

The Trampoline effect

Have you ever watched someone jumping on a trampoline? Initially, the more downward pressure they put on the mat, the farther down they go and the higher they soar!

The way to find the *most* good in our challenges is, from the very beginning, approach them as opportunities to launch us into bigger and better things.

Every person has situations in their life where things seemed to be going bad, bad, bad, and then something good came out of it.

Early in my rabbinic career, I was the rabbi for a very unusual, troubled congregation. The most bizarre things happened in that synagogue. Everything from fistfights breaking out during services to ensuing legal battles between members of the board of directors and the congregation itself. Every day was a new adventure into the darkest side of the organized religious world.

Near the end of that year, my wife and I attended a conference with other young rabbis. As we got together to discuss some of the challenges that we all faced, it became clear that the Almighty was quickly strengthening my metal so I could help my colleagues. My experiences were so ridiculously extreme that I became a source of comfort and perspective for everyone there.

Learn from your experiences

Finding the good in situations becomes a lot easier if we develop an attitude of learning from our mistakes and successes.

The Talmud gives a most potent definition and instruction for a wonderful life.

"Who is wise? He who learns from everyone."

Judaism does not view wisdom as accumulation of facts and formulas. Wisdom is a process that is acquired with a particular attitude. There are smart, successful, happy people in the world; and we can learn a lot from them. There are also foolish, tragic, miserable individuals whom we should learn a lot from as well.

The truly wise person will not only learn from their experiences but will learn from everyone else's too.

One of the advantages of living in a world of Internet and mass media is our exposure to the mistakes, successes, and consequences that befall so many people. A Torah approach to this information is that this is one way the Almighty speaks to us, giving us instruction for how we should live our own lives.

I often wonder how many people adjust their own behavior after a prominent individual is brought to disgrace through his indiscretions.

Do people really become more protective and appreciative of their children after they hear a story of tragedy, or is it just news?

Wise and joyful people are constantly making adjustments to their lives.

> **If you want to experience this more:**
>
> - Look at one person every day for the next month and ask yourself, "What can I learn about life from this person?"
> - Take one news story each day and ask, "What does this teach me about life?"

The time is now!

Every event in our lives holds with it an opportunity. We can allow the event to elevate us, depress us, or just slip by unnoticed.

There is a Jewish holiday called *Shavuos*. It is when we celebrate the revelation of G-d to the entire Jewish People and giving of the Torah and the Ten Commandments to Moses. One year, we were having a community dinner in our synagogue, and I asked the hundred people in attendance to go around the room and share one piece of life wisdom that they had learned in the past year. When the principal of the local Jewish day school's turn came, he declared, "I learned that if you never take the time to ask yourself what you have learned, then you can go a very long time and never realize that you have learned anything."

Put your glasses on!

When my wife was in college, she had a nighttime job at the security desk of one of the buildings on campus. The University of Syracuse was a quiet campus, and she would spend her nights sitting at the desk, studying and doing her homework. One time, her eyes were bothering her and she couldn't wear her contacts or glasses. Her vision is so poor that without glasses she is basically blind. That night, a particularly vulgar individual decided to perform a prank by going up to the desk and flashing his naked body at her. There he stood in front of my wife's desk, dramatically opening his overcoat in front of an innocent co-ed. I still smile when I think of how disappointed the guy must have been when instead of screaming or gasping in shock, my wife simply said, "I can't see anything because I'm not wearing my glasses!" Thank goodness he just took off and ran away!

There are many *wonderful* things around us all the time; and for various reasons, we just can't forget to, or choose not to focus on them. (I'm obviously not referring to that horrible streaker!)

The Good Eye

Ancient Jewish wisdom teaches that one of the most important character traits a person can develop is called "a good eye." On the most basic level, this refers to being tolerant and happy when someone else succeeds. Developing the ability to see the good in people and in all situations is crucial skill to live a happy life. King David remarked in Psalm (128:5). "*And see the good of Jerusalem; even in the holy city, there are negative aspects, but one should have an eye only for the good.*"

The way to do this is to feel satisfied with yourself and your lot in life. It is always easier to rejoice in someone else's success, when you appreciate your own successes and blessings. Such people attract others and become beloved by all, which of course makes it even easier to continue seeing more good in the world.

In my home every Friday night, we have *Shabbos* (Sabbath) dinner. My whole family is present, and often there are several guests. Often, there are more than twenty people around the table. We have a custom in our home to go around the room and have everybody share the "highlight" of their week. This has provided a very efficient structure to catch up on what happened in everyone's lives during the week. It also has trained my children to focus on and appreciate the good in their lives. In addition to this, they have learned to show proper appreciation to those who have been kind to them. If they want their grandparents to take them for ice cream again next week, it is a good idea to thank them publicly for last week's ice cream!

Take a Cardiac Picture

Most times, we let the opportunity of an event escape us. People might spend a year or more, thousands of dollars planning for and fighting over a wedding. Eventually the great day comes . . . and goes, all too quickly. Often, the most vivid memories are the ones captured in the pictures or video. Imagine if you were able to store your positive experiences for another time. This way you could relive them any moment you wanted to. If you were having a lousy day, you would just "plug in" and re-experience the moment.

The way to hold on to the most positive experiences is to take a cardiac picture; store the experience of the event in your heart. Next time you are having an amazing time, stop for a moment and focus on the really good feeling. Then engage as many senses as possible; notice as many details of sight, smell, and sound. Capture them; remember them. Tell yourself that you will revisit every detail of your experience at a later time. Then quickly go back to enjoying the moment.

These very real moments, and memories become your happy places. Anytime you wish to inspire and invigorate yourself, you can revisit those times, become elevated and energized, and go back

Points to remember:

- The most important concept a parent can teach their children is to know that life is good.
- Develop a "good eye" and see the beauty in every situation.
- Accept that life contains a series of daily struggles
- Have patience and look for the good that will come out of the difficult situation.
- Take a cardiac picture to relive positive moments.

Your Notes

Secret # 5

Becoming a True Optimist:

Anticipating a Great Tomorrow

"A pessimist sees the difficulty in every opportunity; an optimist sees the opportunity in every difficulty."

—Winston Churchill

IN ORDER TO live a joyful life, you must become an optimist.

Optimists accomplish more with their time and live happier, healthier, longer lives. They see the world through positive eyes and are always on the lookout for something good around the corner. They often find it too! For the optimist, many times, life becomes a self-fulfilling prophecy.

One reason for that might be because optimism creates enormous amounts of energy, confidence, and inspiration. The result is that optimists seem intent on facing problems head-on, taking active and constructive steps to solve their challenges.

Two kinds of optimists

There are two kinds of optimists: one who is real and one who lives in a world of illusion.

The illusionary is the person who expects that everything will turn out the way that he wants it to be. Clearly, life doesn't work that way. Otherwise, everyone would win the lottery and *always* be healthy; and, of course, children would *always* be a source of pride and pleasure for their parents.

This kind of optimist will have his ups and downs, but I believe he eventually will become jaded and bitter. Having unrealistic expectations is a most certain road to a very dark place. We will talk about the value of expectations a little later.

The real optimist is the person who ultimately expects the best possible outcome from any given situation.

When you walk into the office and say to yourself, "I am going to have a great day. I will be super productive and have an amazing time with it!" You probably will! Like happiness, optimism is completely contagious. You will, de facto, inspire others to succeed more and enjoy their day better as well.

The Joy of potential pleasure

True joy is the anticipation of future good. If you begin to look forward to pleasure coming your way, then you will be amazed at how much joy you will experience. When you anticipate enjoying the beauty in something, you are more likely to see it as beautiful; the joy of it will be more electrifying, more exciting, and more real.

Having a positive attitude is even more productive and easier than being happy. To be happy, you need gratitude for what you have. Joy doesn't require anything! All you need to do is look forward to experiencing pleasure. The looking forward to something is in itself a pleasure.

Is it easier to appreciate what you have now or to look forward to a positive experience in the future?

To live with "Life is Great!" I believe that a person must be proficient in both of these skills. The feeling of satisfaction that one has when they have everything they need is different from the emotion of excitement and anticipation of something good happening in the future.

Always have some thing to look forward to

One time, Rabbi Shmuley Boteach was a guest on my radio show. I asked him to share the most important piece of marriage advice he had for couples. Rabbi Boteach said that every couple should have something to look forward to that they will be doing together.

"I one time did something absolutely marvelous. My wife and I were celebrating our 20th wedding anniversary and we went away to some place very exotic. We stayed at one of the top resorts on the Las Vegas strip. (Even though we live in Las Vegas, we rarely stay in these places.) Once when she was busy getting dressed, I took a pen and paper, and following Rabbi Boteach's advice, I wrote down all of the joyous family occasions that we could possibly look forward to experiencing together over the next 45 years.

I laid it all out in groups. In the next couple of years we could look forward to our youngest son's Bar Mitzvah and our daughter's Bat Mitzvah. After that, we will have another five high school graduations and six college/rabbinical school graduations. Before long, it will be time to dance at the weddings of our six children. I assumed that our children will have the same number of kids that we had. That will mean 36 more brises (ritual circumcisions for the boys) or baby namings (for the girls) for our grand children, and all of their subsequent bar and bat mitzvahs. We aren't done yet! Eventually our grand children will graduate from their schools, get married and start to give us great-grandchildren! The stress of thinking, "How in the world am I going to pay for these 'joyous' occasions?!" quickly dissipated after I handed the list to my wife. Immediately she started to tear up, realizing, that the past 20 years, was just the beginning.

This is a wise piece of advice for everyone in any situation. It is extremely beneficial for a person who is old or sick to have something to look forward to. I know many deathly ill individuals who just "hung in there" for long periods of time because they were anticipating being at a grandchild's wedding or bar mitzvah.

The truth is that everyone should have things they look forward to, goals and aspirations. The more pleasures we can look forward to, the more pleasures we will experience.

If you want to experience this more:

- Anticipate some of the pleasures that you will be feeling in the next hour.
- Identify a challenging situation and visualize it working out well.
- Identify or create an event that you can put on your calendar and look forward to.

What is the best part about being optimistic?

When I posted this question on Facebook, I was flooded with answers. Some of them are as follows:

- *Being able to share it and brighten someone's day without having to do anything but be me.*
- *Believing there is always hope . . .*

And my favorite:

— *The cool secret handshake that we all share.* (I'm thinking; what cool handshake? I'm an optimist, why hasn't anyone told me about this?)

To the extreme, in even the most horrific, tragic situations, keeping a positive attitude can save your life. I once asked Sid, an eighty-six-year-old Holocaust survivor, how he made it through four years in Nazi death camps.

He gave me two answers. The first was that he always did his best to be a kind person. He would try to share a morsel of his bread with someone who needed it, and he used to go into the pits where the corpses were tossed in order to straighten the bodies before they were buried.

The second answer was that he kept a positive attitude and one of faith. People would often talk about how the Germans were going to gather everyone and shoot them. Sid would always protest, "No, we are going to get out of here!" He did. Eventually, Sid was liberated from Auschwitz, got married, and moved to America, where he and his wife raised children and had grandchildren.

Ultimately, the difference between a healthy psyche and one that is not healthy is the ability to know that even the darkest clouds eventually give way to sunshine. It is for this reason that the longest blessing in the Jewish prayer book, that we say everyday, talks about the sun shining and the majesty of the stars. Confidence that there will always be a brighter tomorrow spills over into every area of life.

This too shall pass

There is an ancient Jewish legend about a wise king who sent his son on a very long mission to the farthest part of the kingdom. He gave the prince a magical ring with the words, "This Too Shall Pass" written on it. When the prince encountered difficulties, he would read the words and be encouraged that the difficulties were just temporary. When the prince was experiencing pleasure and success, he looked at the words and would be reminded not to take his successes for granted. He appreciated every pleasure because he understood that, it too shall pass.

I found this to be a very profound insight into personal happiness. Keeping in mind this saying of "This Too Shall Pass" can establish a kind of equilibrium for your emotions. When teaching this material in a seminar, I would open the discussion by having people rate their personal happiness with a number between one and ten. Ten being so happy that you are just flying high and one being so miserable that you want to put a bullet in your head.

Most people seem to naturally to exist somewhere in the middle between the high and low numbers, depending on what is going on in their lives at the time. The problem with this is that many times after a great high there is often a deep low. Think of your wedding or graduation for example. The next day there is a letdown. It is not that there is anything wrong with today, but compared to the excitement of yesterday, it can be just a little blah.

Recognizing the temporal nature of life's situations gives a stability that I find very helpful for personal happiness. Instead of having your happiness rating go from a 9 to a 3, back to an 8 then a 2. "This Too Shall Pass" can help you stay at a pretty good 7.5 a lot longer.

"This Too Shall Pass" is not only a helpful psychological tool, but I believe that it is an accurate statement of the cycles of life. We find in the Bible that Joseph oversaw seven years of plenty followed by seven years famine. This story is to inform us about the cyclical nature of everything from agriculture to economics and politics.

Next time a business deal goes bad or your political candidate doesn't make it into office, you probably don't have to sweat it out too much. Just remind yourself that soon the cycle will begin again and that this too shall pass.

Being optimistic increases value

Imagine for a moment that you turn on the news and find out that all the future economic indicators are crashing down. (This is completely hypothetical of course!) What would happen to your stock portfolio?

Imagine you turn on the news and it showed investors coming out of the woodwork like crazy, talking about how much money everyone is about to make. What would happen to your stock portfolio then?

In reality, nothing has changed except people's expectation of what will happen. When we visualize things going well, we become hopeful and energetic. Our natural creativity and resourcefulness comes out, and our world expands. When our mind's eye does not focus on the good that is around the corner, we become tired, ineffective, and we enter a contraction mode. Things that we used to do with ease become difficult, and it becomes harder to enjoy even the simple pleasures of life.

Sam and Barbara had what they considered an "okay" marriage. They had been together for seven years and had no children. In their relationship there was some good, more bad, but the good was so good that it was worth it. Life was just kind of rolling along until one day, Barbara got pregnant! They were both ecstatic. They came to me beaming with anticipation of raising a family, looking for ways to improve their marriage.

The prospect of raising children infused new value into their relationship. They started to learn what Judaism had to say about marriage and really started improving their communication and appreciation of each other. Happily, today, they have two children and a fantastic marriage.

Being optimistic about the future and living with a positive attitude increases the value of everything in our lives.

If you want to experience this more:

- Pick an area of your life, and for two minutes a day, visualize it getting better and better. Imagine details of your success beyond what you have experienced in the past.
- Find a "role model," someone who has accomplished what you wish to accomplish. Ask yourself or, better yet, ask them, "What did they do to get where they are today?"
- Implement some of those ideas into your life and continue to visualize your growth.

Is there a danger in being too optimistic?

Living like life is great, requires us to be constantly looking forward to good things happening. One can never over envision the best case scenarios from occurring. That is precisely what it means to be an optimist! However, we all know that sometimes, things just don't work out as planned. In order prevent ourselves from creating a stream of disappointments and unrealized expectations; we have to monitor how much idealism we infuse in our daily lives. How much good should we look forward to?

I have found in my own life and in many whom I have counseled, that increasing our vision of expectancy by 10 percent increments is effective and realistic.

An Optimist + 10% = A Realist

One should identify the best possible outcome of any situation and then add 10 percent. Visualize your spouse being 10 percent more loving, making 10 percent more money than the best possible scenario for your business, and being 10 percent happier than you ever thought you could be.

Few things can make a person more miserable than a life filled with unrealized expectations.

This is why you have to find a balance between looking forward to a life of blessings and keeping your expectations in check.

The way you do this is by distinguishing between things that are up to you and things that are beyond your control.

Keep your self-expectations high! Expect to enjoy your day; expect to see beauty in every person you meet. Expect that you should feel many different pleasures and that, in an overall sense, life will be wonderful. Expect to love yourself even after you don't meet your self-expectations. All these things are dependent only on *your* attitudes.

Expect *nothing* from anyone else.

Don't expect gratitude. Don't expect kindness. Don't expect loyalty.

The more we expect from others, the more we will be disappointed. However, if you really, really have no expectations from other people, there will be many times in life that you will be pleasantly surprised. The lower our expectations of others are, the more gratitude we will have for them when they do something nice for us.

The only exception to this is that children need to expect that they will be loved and taken care of by their parents until they are adults. Unfortunately, we live in a world where both parents often work to make ends meet. The result is that many children, when they are young, are raised in day care centers or by people other than their parents. This is not beneficial for most children's "security quotient." A security quotient refers to how secure a person feels. Before the age of 5, the most important thing to impart to children is that they are loved and will never be left alone. Parents who spend more time with their infants and toddlers create happier, more secure, more trusting people. The older children get, the more they mature and become independent, and the need for constant attention decreases.

Spoiling Effect

Anytime a person allows themselves to develop a sense of entitlement, they do themselves and the people around them a tremendous disservice. Entitlement is the active enemy of gratitude and destroyer of positive attitudes.

When you get what you feel you are entitled to, you aren't happy because you were expecting it.

When you *don't* get what you feel you are entitled to, you are disappointed at best, but you are more likely to feel infuriated! Why? Because you didn't get what you felt you had coming to you!

There are many parents who want to give everything to their children. In the process, they end up spoiling them. The word *spoiling* is so interesting because it conjures a vision of a beautiful banana that quickly got mashed and turned all brown. In the quest to give children the best of everything, often parents create an attitude of entitlement in their children. This actually works against their goal and prevents their children from learning to appreciate their gifts and blessings.

The way to prevent the "spoiling effect" from creeping into your children is to

a. have them earn their luxuries through chores or meaningful accomplishments;
b. make sure they have friends who have "less" than they do.

This way, your children will not think that they have anything coming to them and will appreciate more what they do get.

What children should always be able to expect is that their parents will love them and be there for them when they are needed. In this way, we may nurture and develop secure, happy, and appreciative individuals.

Points to remember:

- The optimist expects the best possible outcome from any given situation.
- True joy is the anticipation of future good.
- Always have something to look forward to.
- This Too Shall Pass
- Being optimistic increases value.
- Keep your expectations of yourself high and expect *nothing* from anyone else.

Your Notes

Secret # 6

Got Gratitude?

Appreciating What You Have

The definition of wealth

"Who is wealthy? One who rejoices in his portion."

THE PATH TO true happiness is appreciating what we have rather than focusing on what we do not have.

Or in the words of a famous Sheryl Crow song, "It's not having what you want, it's wanting what you've got."

Everybody knows someone who has more things than they do and are less happy than them, and we all know people that have a lot less stuff than us and *they* are happier than we are.

Once we have our basic needs taken care of, personal happiness has very little to do with *how much* we have and has a lot to do with our ability to appreciate *whatever we do* have.

Just noticing what you have is half the battle

One of my teachers, Rabbi Zelig Pliskin, relates the story in his book, *Gateway to Happiness*, of a man who one day decided to spend a few minutes appreciating his morning cup of coffee. He was a coffee enthusiast. If he wanted to stop drinking coffee he could at any time; he just didn't want to stop drinking! It was part of his daily routine; and if G-d forbid, he ever had to go without it, he would really miss it. As he began to ponder the miracle of his morning brew, he first thought about how the beans were grown in Brazil, someone had to plant the trees and tend them to maturity. Workers had to pick the beans, roast them, pack and ship them to the states. There was tremendous work involved in the shipping industry, which allowed the coffee to reach the United States—this alone required hundreds if not thousands of people. Finally, the coffee beans arrived in his grocery store. But that was not all, the water for the coffee was boiled on a gas range, and the story of the manufacture and delivery of that appliance into his kitchen could easily fill a book. Then there was the gas and the water that magically was produced and delivered through pipes to his home. The milk required reflection on an entire dairy industry to explain how it made it's way from the cow to the farm, to the processing plant, to the store, into his car, and finally into his coffee. The sugar that every day was habitually mixed into his cup had a similar story. The man didn't even begin to describe the cup he used or the table and chair that he sat on while he enjoyed his morning beverage.

For the first time he recognized the thousands of people and their efforts that aided him in his one cup of coffee. This awareness led him to a very spiritual experience and he was permeated with a profound feeling of gratitude for the next few weeks.

If you want to experience this more:

- Go through the same exercise with one of your simple, everyday pleasures. Ask yourself how it got to you and reflect on how many people and steps it took to get to you so that you can enjoy it.

The curse of comparing what we have to others

A friend of mine, Rabbi Yitz Greenman, tells of an experience that really concretizes this idea. One time, he and his family spent a few weeks during the summer in a modest bungalow in the Catskills. Compared to their regular home, it was a little better than a shack, yet everybody loved it. He asked a senior rabbi, Rabbi Reuven Feinstein, "How can it be that we love the bungalow but we find so many faults with our houses that are a hundred times more valuable and furnished?"

"It's simple," he said. "If it weren't for the neighbors, everyone would be happy with what they have. Here in the mountains, everyone is living in run-down shacks, and there's nothing better to compare it to—yet it's enough because in reality, it is enough. But at home there are many different houses on the block. Some are nicer and have bigger backyards. As we compare ours with the others', we tell ourselves that what we have is not enough. That's how people make themselves miserable."

I believe that Rabbi Feinstein is right. We all have more than enough to live. But we tell ourselves that it's not enough because we constantly are comparing what we have with our neighbors. We are trying to keep up with the Joneses.

When we compare what we have to others, it is more difficult to appreciate what we have

My wife and I once attended a small party in a physician's home in the nicest neighborhood in Las Vegas. In a quiet moment on the side, our host was lamenting to us on all his financial woes. My wife and I had just moved into a new home and were really happy with it. As we were leaving, she commented on how his house was literally three times the size of ours and compared to his house, ours was a slum. "How could he have the audacity to complain to us like that?" my wife said, "Look at his house! It's a palace!". I replied, "Yes, but look at what he sees every morning when he leaves for work. Each property is more magnificent than the next. Everyday, he has to face the fact that, in this neighborhood, he is the poorest kid on the block."

The Tenth commandment; "Thou shalt not covet!"

Last but certainly not the least, now we can understand the wisdom behind the commandment not to covet your neighbor's house, wife, donkey, or anything else that is his. Besides simply not being nice, coveting other people's possessions' is counterproductive to personal happiness. When we focus on what other people have and desire it, we can't appreciate what we have.

This is why the Talmud explains that when unbridled, "jealousy, desire, and quest for honor, remove a person from this world."

Each of these three traits contains a quality that makes it impossible to focus on the pleasures available to us right now.

Let gratitude be your attitude!

There is a story of a man who once contracted a rare, untreatable disease of the eyes that caused complete blindness. After he lost his sight, an unusually skilled doctor visited him with an experimental treatment that had the potential to restore the man's vision. The anticipation for the procedure was great. After the treatment and recovery, the man's sight had returned better than before! Imagine the joy and appreciation that this man has for his eyesight.

Have you ever lost your glasses and then, after a long while, found them?

The truly wise and happy individual appreciates his blessings before he loses them.

I went to school with a guy who occasionally would blindfold himself for an entire day just to develop a greater appreciation for his eyesight.

Another friend of mine would go for periods of time, a few hours or more, without speaking anything other than the Torah so that he would appreciate his ability to converse.

> **If you want to experience this more:**
>
> - Take three things that you use and enjoy in everyday life and intentionally abstain from them for a longer period of time than usual. For example, stop drinking coffee for two days (Just kidding; let's leave the coffee out of this!), no phone or computer for an entire day. Try not to spend any money or use credit cards for two days in a row.

One time, when teaching this point in a class, several people stood up and testified that their observance of the Jewish Sabbath had just this effect. For one day a week they weren't using their phones, doing household chores, watching TV, shopping or smoking. During the day they felt completely free of the pressures of life, but at the end of the twenty-five-hour Sabbath, they appreciated their normal activities in a whole different way.

Even if we have *very* little, we can still appreciate it

Principles in wisdom are often found in the most extreme cases.

Ernie is an eighty-six-year-old Holocaust survivor. He explained to me that sometimes he can can get a little depressed or discouraged, but those feelings do not stay with him very long. When he was in Auschwitz, one of his "jobs" was to feed the Germans' guard dogs. After feeding the dogs, he was allowed to scrape the remains of dog food from the dogs' bowls and eat. He told me that those were the best meals he ate during those years.

When Ernie starts feeling down, he then looks back at his life and how much he appreciated the little he had. He looks at his life now;

after being liberated, he got married, raised children, built a business, and has lived a healthy life. He asks himself, "Is there any stress or problem that is worth staying depressed over?"

Appreciating what we *don't* have

It should go without saying that we should thank our lucky stars every day that we don't have cancer or some other terrible ailment. The fact that my children aren't on drugs and I have a job to go to every morning is nothing to take for granted. There are many greater, more righteous people than I, who have fallen on hard times and have had difficult challenges.

What about the good things that we don't have? Should we really be grateful for not having them?

Sarah was a kind woman with very modest needs. It wasn't a situation that her husband's *net* income didn't meet up with their *gross* habits. They kept their lifestyle expenses minimal, and yet there was just never enough money to go around. It was an underlying source of constant tension in the home.

One day, she heard that a friend of her husband was indicted for tax-evasion and fraud. They had come into some money, bought a business, and seemed to be doing very well. Evidently, there was some pretty shady stuff going on.

Just then, Sarah had an epiphany that she shared with her husband. She said, "I don't think that we are more righteous or moral than they are. We have never been tested with having money like that, but maybe if we were, we would have done the same things as they did. Instead of being frustrated that we are poor, maybe we should be more grateful that we aren't tested like that by being rich."

Through Sarah's humility, she learned to appreciate even the things that she did not have.

Do you need anything to be happy other than a great attitude?

Just to reiterate something that I said in the introduction of this book, Judaism rejects the notion that a person can be happy for no reason at all. Everyone needs to recognize that they have a certain amount of blessings in their life. We all possess a limited portion of talent, money, health, love, and opportunity. Personal happiness is dependent on our ability to rejoice over and appreciate that portion.

Sometimes it is easy to see your good portion. My father-in-law of blessed memory, used to always say, "If you have your health, you have your wealth!" Having a job or being married with children are blessings that people can appreciate every day.

However, sometimes our blessings are difficult to recognize because there are so many challenges distracting us. It is similar to speaking on your phone in a crowded public place. There are times you need to get to a different spot so the background noise doesn't interfere with you hearing the other person.

Jessica is a woman who has a drug addiction problem. After twenty years of going in and out of jail and rehab, the state was finally about to take away her two very young children. I was able to find an incredible family to adopt both siblings. With tears in her eyes and agony in her heart, she watched as her children went to their new home.

It was a very bitter pill to take, knowing that she would not raise her children as their mother. However, beneath all the pain, Jessica realized how blessed she was. Her children would have a loving, responsible home to grow up in, and she would still have access to them as they grew up. Jessica came to understand that this "portion" that G-d gave her was something to truly rejoice over.

Even though one's portion may not seem desirable at the time, when examined closely enough with a broader perspective, often there are many things to appreciate.

Life is about pleasure!

As we stated before, the concept of monotheism that the Jewish people brought to the world, includes the idea that G-d created humanity only for its own pleasure and enjoyment.

It is obvious that life is filled with bountiful pleasures and Ancient Jewish wisdom teaches us that it is our obligation to enjoy them. It is so important that the Kabbalah stresses that one of the questions we will have to answer before the heavenly throne when we die will be, "Did you benefit from all of the permissible pleasures of this world?"

There was a great rabbi who lived in Germany in the 1800s. When he was getting older and becoming frail, he arranged to go on a trip to Switzerland. People started asking him why he was going, he responded that after he died, he didn't want to stand before G-d as the Almighty would say to him, "Rabbi Shimshon, I put you on this earth for eighty years and you didn't bother to go see my Alps!"

The Five Classes of Pleasure

Ancient Jewish wisdom teaches us that there are five classes of pleasure that are available to all of us every day of our lives. If we know and are aware of what they are and when they are available to us, we are more likely to experience them. The trick is to focus and appreciate each one, starting from the lowest, most easily attainable, graduating to the highest:

Fifth class: Physical pleasures

These are pleasures that we experience through our five senses—sight, sound, touch, taste, and smell. Taking a hot shower on a cold morning and enjoying the sensation of the water flowing over you, drinking your first cup of coffee and experiencing the bitterness and sweetness at the same time, wearing a fine piece of clothing, the purely physical pleasure of sexual relations, listening to music while you exercise, feeling the movement of your body. These are all intense pleasures and are available to us at almost every moment of our lives. In many universities, you can take a course in wine tasting in order to learn how to fully appreciate that particular pleasure.

The purpose of these pleasures is to give us energy in order to acquire deeper, more meaningful pleasures.

Every pleasure has a counterfeit; like a counterfeit $100 bill, it might look and feel like money, but it isn't money.

When a person becomes so involved in physical pleasure that it is wiping them out or it becomes an addiction, they are no longer involved in the pleasure but in the counterfeit.

> **If you want to experience this more:**
>
> - Take one simple physical pleasure, and while you are experiencing it, notice as many details as you can: What is the temperature and texture? Is it sweet or bitter, smooth or silky? The more aspects you can identify, the better.

Fourth class: The Pleasure of Love

Love is probably one of the most used and most nebulously defined words in the English language. If you enjoy watching people experience just a little discomfort, ask them to first use, and then define the word *love*.

Jewish wisdom has a clear definition.

Love is the emotional feeling one gets when they identify and appreciate the virtues in another.

When we focus on what is special about a person, we increase our appreciation for them. When we focus on what is special about ourselves, we increase our appreciation and love of ourselves.

When we focus on what is virtuous and beautiful about a person, in spite of their faults, we are filled with pleasure. That pleasure is what we call love. The more we know about a person, the more we can love them. One cannot love a book they have not yet read, and we can't love a person that we don't know.

There are those who say that "love is blind."

I disagree. Love is the ultimate magnifying glass. Ask someone who loves them the most and they will often answer, "My mother." Now ask them who knows their faults better than anyone else, they will often say again, "My mother."

The reason people make the mistake of thinking that love is blind is that they are confusing love with its counterfeit pleasure, infatuation. Infatuation has a lot to do with desire and very little to do with the genuine recognition of who someone is. Desire causes us to, at best, overlook the faults and, at worst, view the faults as "cute and adorable." Somehow, the faults become part of what makes the person so right!

The feeling of love is greatly enhanced after we bestow goodness to someone. When we give of ourselves, our time, or our money, a part of us becomes part of that person. We begin to identify with them in a more intimate way.

One of the reasons most of us love our children more than we love our spouses is because we spend so much time and energy giving to our children. Our most intense love should be with our spouse, but it usually isn't; after scouring the world looking at another two billion females, we did choose to marry that one particular woman. My kids are just a product of my marriage. However, because children, from the time they are born, require so much from their parents, we give to them and end up loving them more deeply. People divorce their spouses all the time; they almost never divorce their children. There is simply too much invested in our kids to do that.

If I want to increase the amount of love I have for a person, not only should I focus on their virtues, but I should start giving to them more often and more significantly.

Love is obviously a much deeper pleasure than any of the physical pleasures we feel. Betty had just learned that her husband Eddie was having an affair. Betty came to me in tears and completely distraught; the fact that she had just bought a new BMW was of no consolation to her.

In as much as love is a deeper pleasure, it is also much more difficult to appreciate than any physical pleasure.

Imagine Mr. Schwartz, a successful investment banker who works long hours in order to reach a financial plateau of $10 million. His goal is to retire with his family in comfort. Suppose someone offers Mr. Schwartz $10 million in exchange for one of his children. The buyer promises to take good care of the child and reminds Schwartz that he will be able to retire right now! The only drawback is that Schwartz can never see or talk to his child again. Would Mr. Schwartz take the offer? (It might depend on if the child is a teenager!)

Schwartz tells his secretary to cancel the next two days of appointments so that he can spend more time with his family. He goes home early that night just in time for his wife to quickly hand him a crying baby. Then she asks him to bathe a toddler, and read *Babar Goes to the Circus* to their other child. After reading *Babar* for the seventeenth time in one day, is it any wonder why Schwartz is ready to go back to the office?

What is Schwartz's problem? He needs a course in *love tasting* in order to learn how to fully love and appreciate his children.

Infatuation and misdirected love are counterfeits to fourth class of pleasure. Infatuation is the focus on what the person represents, not who the person is. Loving a person because they are famous good-looking or have a great job are examples of this.

There is a story of a man who always spoke about how much he "loved" fish. One time, he went fishing and caught a gorgeous sea bass. As he was devouring it, he exclaimed, "I love fish!" A friend of his said, "If you really loved the fish, you would have taken it home, fed it, and put it into a big aquarium. You don't love fish. You love eating it. You love yourself!"

People often claim they love others when what they really love is what others do for them; they just love themselves!

> **If you want to experience this more:**
>
> - Identify two people that you love and write down all the reasons you love them.
> - Next time you meet someone for the first time, try after a few minutes, to identify as many virtues as you can in them.

Third Class: The Pleasure of being good and living with purpose

This next class of pleasures is even more intense than love. In this pleasure, love even takes the backseat. People will leave their families and go to war. Stay late at work and be away from their families in order to provide for them.

Why? Every one of us has a deep desire for purpose in our lives. If you ever have felt that "what is my life about anyway?" feeling, it is because at that moment you were not connected with third class pleasure.

This pleasure is living with meaning and doing the right thing. It is such a powerful pleasure that people will literally give up their lives for it. Imagine if someone came to you with this dilemma: They put a gun to your head and said, "You must kill a thousand innocent children or I am going to kill you!" What would you do? If you are like any of the thousands of people I've asked this question to, you will take the bullet rather than kill the children. Why? Most people say, "Because killing is wrong." I ask, "Haven't you done anything 'wrong' before?" They answer that this is just "*too* wrong." People are willing to die to be "good."

As my mentor, Rabbi Noah Weinberg, often said, "If being good is worth dying for, then it is worth living for. And if something is valuable enough to die *and* to live for, then it is certainly worth enjoying."

The problem is that doing the right thing and living a meaningful life often come with a price that makes living them very difficult. The price is couched in a moral conflict or dilemma.

A person who is desperately trying to lose weight may say, "I know that I'm on a diet, but today is a special occasion. As a matter of fact, I once heard the rabbi say that we should treat every day like a special occasion!" So the battle continues, every time they break their diet, their self-esteem takes a beating. When they are successful, they feel great about themselves and experience an increase in self-respect.

The more difficult the challenge, the more potential there is for feeling third-class pleasure.

Let's say Sally was once sitting on a park bench. She looked down and saw an envelope. At that exact moment, someone ran towards her and said, "Oh, I dropped that." Immediately after Sally handed her the envelope, the grateful woman opened it and told Sally, with a smile of relief, that her life savings of ten thousand dollars were still in it.

Now imagine that YOU are sitting at a park bench for about a half hour and not one person has passed by. You look down and find an envelope with ten thousand dollars. You tell yourself you will give it another thirty minutes to see if anyone comes by. At the end of the thirty minutes, you start to leave the park and in your mind you have just finished spending most of the money. Right then, a guy comes running up to you. He is panic-stricken, and sweat drips from his brow. He asks if you have seen an envelope near the bench over there. You hand him the envelope and ask, "Is this what you were looking for?" How do you feel now? Who is a better person, you or Sally? If you're feeling a little rage and frustration, then you need a course in *doing-the-right-thing tasting*.

What could be a counterfeit pleasure for doing good?

There are three common counterfeits of third class of pleasure:

1. Being dedicated to a cause that is inherently not very meaningful
2. Misdirecting kindness towards others
3. Creating an undeserved high self-esteem

As the depth of each pleasure increases, so does the confusion and potential destruction with it's counterfeit. I will now briefly address why each of these is something to be wary of.

Being dedicated to the wrong cause

One time I was called to pay a visit to an elderly couple's home. When I arrived, I was shocked to find eight living cats and another two hundred-plus statues of cats. As it turns out, the man spent his life involved in his business and his wife never had children. Therefore she devoted all of her time and money to the preservation of cats. Now she is in her mid-seventies and is confused why she is feeling that her life has been empty.

I have nothing against animals or pets. I grew up and also raised my children with pets. Lots of pets, at one time we had six cats and some other creatures in our house! They can provide comfort, an object to bestow love upon, and assistance for those in need. However, the point is to find the *most* meaningful causes to put our energies into.

The whales have done a lot for the world, no question, and they should be saved. However, the Jewish people have done even more and also deserved to be helped.

Things being equal, a person should devote their time and resources to those things that will bring the most amounts of good in the world and things that they have been steered towards. If you were born into a particular country or religion, first look into strengthen those causes. If a family member suffers from an ailment, it might be that the Almighty is guiding you to help that particular cause.

Third-class pleasure plays such an important role in personal happiness, that a significant part of "Secret # 7: Living a Meaningful Life: Finding Your Greater Purpose" will be dedicated to it.

For now, you will greatly benefit by making a decision to enjoy doing the right thing and to dedicate yourself to finding more meaningful activities to be involved with.

Misdirecting kindness

Whoever is kind to the cruel will end up being cruel to the kind.

—*the Talmud*

Ancient Jewish wisdom teaches that within each of us, there is a desire to do good and a desire to do bad. Rarely are we subject to making mistakes because we follow the desire to do bad things. I highly doubt that you have ever woken up one morning with a desire to rape, murder, or steal and have followed through with that impulse. However, there are many people who wish to be kind or merciful to others, when they, in fact, should rebuke or discipline.

I have counseled many parents who, in the interest of their children's happiness, did not insist on forcing their kids to do their schoolwork. In the end, it was their children who lose out when they don't have proper study habits and could not succeed academically.

A friend of mine recently witnessed a large family fortune dwindle to almost nothing because he did not want to hurt his employees by laying them off. Even though his business was hemorrhaging money, he couldn't fathom the thought of causing his employees pain by telling his them that they would need to find work elsewhere. True, he did manage to keep tens of his friends employed during and economic down turn; but it was at the expense of what his father had built during his lifetime and the potential opportunities he could have given his children.

Not only is it important to be kind but one also has to be clear on what is considered true kindness and to whom is their first priority. If we are confused about this, then this counterfeit pleasure could bring a lot of heartache to those we actually care for the most.

Creating an undeserved high self-esteem

Having a high sense of self is a very important quality that should be nurtured on a daily basis. The Kabbala explains that the root of self-worth should be that we are created in the image of G-d. This should inspire us to behave in a holy way. Just like G-d is kind, merciful, and so on, so to we should train ourselves to be kind, merciful, and so on. Ancient Jewish wisdom maintains that we are the children of G-d, and in the same manor that a prince holds himself up to honor his father the king, we too should behave in a way that brings honor to our Father the King. This is real self-esteem and very valuable for living a meaningful, happy life.

The confusion is when people lavish undeserved praise and accolades on others. Besides being an actual prohibition in the Torah, it creates a false sense of self. One might think that if I keep telling people that they are fabulously good without having them deserve it, they will become fabulously good.

In fact, the opposite is true. There is no correlation between goodness and high self-esteem. However, there is a correlation between criminality and high self-esteem.

Florida State University Professor Roy Baumeister (PhD psychology, Princeton University) has revealed that in a lifetime of study of violent criminals, the one characteristic nearly all these criminals share is high self-esteem.

It is remarkable; people with high self-esteem are the ones most prone to violence. If you think about it, it actually makes sense. In most cases, it would take a lot of gumption to put a gun to another person's head and rob a convenience store.

When we lavish undeserved praise on others, we create egos that need to be fed. In the quest to make oneself higher on the totem pole, it is almost always easier to knock someone else down rather than climb yourself.

When we praise others who deserve recognition, it strengthens them and inspires them to do more good. When we praise those who don't deserve it, at best it isn't helpful in there development and most probably it will be very destructive.

If you want to experience this more:

- Think of a time you did the right thing without thinking about it. Now focus on the pleasure of knowing that you are good.
- Think of a time when you did the right thing and it was very challenging for you. Now focus on the pleasure of knowing that you are *very* good.
- Identify one time when your inclination to do good has gotten you in trouble and watch out!

Second Class: The pleasure of Power

The best way to illustrate this pleasure is through its counterfeit. What will inspire some to kill thousands of innocent people? Power.

Hitler, Stalin, and Pol Pot all killed millions of people while solidifying control over their regimes.

The real pleasure these people were looking for is the ability to create. An architect or builder can experience this. Have you ever met a talented musician or artist? Intuitively, they know that they have something over the rest of us, and they do! When they use their abilities to create, they are connecting with the Divine. One of the deepest pleasures of parenting is taking a little baby who does a lot of screaming and pooping, and training them to be a mature, responsible, and independent person.

It is different from love. Love is the pleasure attained by appreciating the virtue and beauty in your children. This is the pleasure achieved by influencing them in a positive way.

One of my favorite questions to ask people is; "What pleasure do you get from your profession?"

I have inquired from several past and present governors on what exactly is their pleasure in holding office. They all have responded in a similar vein. "If I want the bathroom painted green, it gets painted green." When I asked some of them how their experience as governor differed from their experience as a senator or congressman, again they all had similar answers. "In Congress you are one of hundreds. You spend your time convincing others to do things your way. As governor, you just do what you want." Now we all know that, even as a head of a state government, you don't just do what you want. However, they are connecting with the pleasure of power.

Why is this level of pleasure so special?

Having a creative influence over people and events is a way to emulate the Almighty. The ultimate expression of creativity was G-d's creation of the world. He made something from absolutely nothing. Expressing our own creativity is a taste of that power.

However, because it is such a deep pleasure, a person must often push themselves to their limits in order to fully experience the feelings of power or being creative. The opportunities are rarer, and the counterfeits are numerous. Exerting control through oppressive manipulation is a good example of this kind of counterfeit pleasure.

In order to steer away from the counterfeits, you have to develop a real clarity of life.

How can you distinguish between the real pleasures of creativity and its counterfeits of control and manipulation?

Look at the results. Proper creativity gives other people pleasure. It leads them to lives that are more productive and fulfilling. Control through oppressive manipulation may, in the short term, yield results but eventually leads to destruction.

If you want to get your young child to stop doing something, one of the most effective ways is to hit them. You will get their attention and they will stop. The problem with that form of behavior modification is as soon as you leave, they will probably get back to doing the wrong thing. A better parenting strategy is to develop a system of positive reinforcement and education. Try and show your children that it is in their best interest to behave in a certain way, and they will adopt that as a lifestyle.

The Kabbah teaches this point by expressing a parable of a tree. How do you know if a fruit tree is healthy? Taste its fruits. If they are sweet, it is a healthy tree. A person should constantly monitor what they produce in this world. Whether I'm producing children, friendships, or business alliances, I should always make sure that they are sweet.

In this way, I can be assured that I am involved in the right kind of influence.

> **If you want to experience this more:**
>
> - Identify ways that you are enriching your life or the lives of others.
> - Look at the people you influence and project how your actions will affect them in the future.

First class: The Love of G-d

The essence of this is the recognition that every pleasure we experience is an aspect of the Almighty.

Feeling a cool breeze on the back of your neck on a hot day, *kevelling* (absorbing intense pleasure) over your children when they are sleeping, or feeling great about helping someone out; all these are pleasures in and of themselves. When we connect them to the Creator and master of the universe, it launches us into an experience of holiness and awe.

First-class pleasure—love of G-d—means getting in touch with the absolute awesomeness of life. An amazing sunset, peering into the stars, the birth of a baby: these are moments wherein we feel something beyond ourselves.

It doesn't happen often, but when it does, the power is immense. It takes our breath away.

Awe is the experience of merging our small, relatively insignificant selves with something much greater. We break beyond our own limitations and connect with the unity of G-d.

G-d is the creator and source of everything. Jewish tradition teaches that we are in a state of constant recreation. He is ever present and ever involved.

Every pleasure that we feel is an opportunity to feel G-d's presence and to know him better.

Imagine someone who has mastered the first four classes of pleasure. Every day they enjoy and appreciate all the physical pleasures they come across. They interact with their beautiful, loving family and are driven with purpose and meaning in life; they are creative and they use all their power to bring good in the world. Yet there's still something missing.

An encounter with the infinite: an encounter with G-d.

No human being is totally satisfied unless they are in touch with the transcendent dimension.

There are bodily pleasures and there are soul pleasures. If we don't eat, no matter how spiritual we may be, we will feel a craving, then pain, then sickness. It is similar with the soul pleasures. No matter how much physical pleasure we experience, we will crave the G-d experience. Most people aren't necessarily aware that this is what they are going for. Often we distract ourselves with all sorts of things—some worthwhile, some not. When all is said and done, what we all seek is to reach out of this finite world and connect with the infinite. To become one with G-d.

This is one of the main reasons, many people feel that it is so important to have someone to carry on the family name. Most people do this through their children, but some put their names on buildings or find other worthwhile projects to immortalize themselves. We desire to leave something in this world that will outlive our existence. It is a very natural desire to be eternal. That is also why mystery, magic, and miracles capture our imaginations. They impel us to break beyond our own limitations.

The pleasure of feeling the love of G-d is incomparable to any other experience we have. Nothing finite, nothing bound up in this world can compare to the infinite. Next to love of G-d, all other pleasures are insignificant. We can have delicious pizza, lots of money, love, and power. But humans long to transcend the mundane reality of daily living.

> **If you want to experience this more:**
>
> - First meditate on the oneness of G-d. Think about how he created and runs the world. Feel his presence with you right now.
> - Next, identify pleasures that you are experiencing. Think of them as gifts from the Almighty and use your gratitude to lift your emotions to a state of awe.
>
> I did not say that this would be easy! However, with practice, feeling the pleasure of the love of G-d is definitely attainable on a regular basis.

Why don't we focus on our pleasures?

There are four major reasons that we don't enjoy our pleasures to the fullest.

1) Often we get caught up in our worries and frustrations of daily life and they distract us from focusing on our pleasures.

   Imagine going into a restaurant and, when presented with the bill, saying, "I'll pay twice this amount, thank you!" This is what worry is. I anticipate things going wrong, perhaps at a family dinner. So I spend an hour (usually more!) "paying" or suffering over something that has not yet occurred. Then the event happens. Either everything works out fine, in which case I needlessly suffer or "pay" for a dinner that I didn't even eat. If things really did go bad, I pay double—once before the event and once during the lousy time.

I actually end up paying a third time. Worry and acceptance of frustration, like happiness, are habit-forming. Once I start doing it, it is increasingly easier to continue. Worrying begets worrying, and frustration begets frustration.

2) Many of the pleasures we have had our whole lives, so we get used to them and take them for granted.

As one of my rabbis taught me, the difference between a luxury and a necessity is that a necessity *is* a luxury that we got used to. My morning coffee used to be a cup of Israeli instant. Then I started going to 7-Eleven before prayers. Now if it isn't Starbucks or Coffee Bean & Tea Leaf, I won't touch it!

3) We trick ourselves into thinking that things are lousy today because things were really good before.

Sam was a middle-aged professional who came to speak with me when he was feeling down. I asked him to share with me some of his major complaints about life. He told me that his stock portfolio was down 60 percent from the previous year, he slipped a disk in his back, and his son and grandchildren moved to the other side of the country.

Now imagine Sam was in prison for the past ten years. He had no money, he had been beaten and assaulted repeatedly, and his kids wanted nothing to do with him. Puff! He finds himself in the exact situation that he is in today. All of a sudden that small stock portfolio doesn't look so bad. Only a slipped disk? No problem! He is also planning his next trip to visit the kids, who still call him a couple of times a week.

Sam was comparing yesterday to today, and yes, today does not look as rosy. If he would look at today independent of any other time, he could appreciate the many blessings that immediately lie before him.

4) The Kabbala teaches us that ingratitude is the most basic spiritual test that every human must deal with.

   Starting with the first man, Adam, in the Garden of Eden after he ate the fruit that was forbidden to him by G-d. G-d asked Adam, "Did you eat from the tree that I told you not to eat from?" Adam's response was "G-d, the woman that YOU gave to me, gave me the fruit and I ate it."

   In other words, "G-d, it is YOUR fault that I ate from the tree. If YOU had not given her to me, then I never would have eaten."

   Instead of appreciating the greatest gift that was ever given to him, his wife, Adam threw the whole thing back on the Almighty.

   Obviously, G-d knew that Adam and Eve had eaten the fruit, so why did He ask the question? G-d was hoping that Adam would 'fess up and take responsibility for his actions. He didn't appreciate what G-d had done for him, and therefore, it was easy for him to avoid taking responsibility.

   From that time onward, ingratitude was placed in our spiritual DNA as it were. In order to live happy, joyful lives, we need to fight against this aspect of our nature and become grateful to all who have helped us and for all the pleasures we experience.

The cure for ingratitude and pathway to appreciation

The Happiness Game ☺

One of best ways to train ourselves in gratitude is by playing "the happiness game."

Write down a list of ten things that you are grateful for right now. People often start with things like health, family, job . . . Tomorrow, add another three items to the list and continue every day for one month. You cannot repeat items, but you can become more specific. So you might start off appreciating your health, but as the month progresses, you will work your way to thanking G-d for your left knee and only mildly high cholesterol.

I have seen this exercise work wonders in my life and the lives of many others. Eventually, you can develop a habit of focusing on your blessings and becoming a very positive person.

If you want to experience this more:

- Create a vision of your entire day incorporating the five levels of pleasure.
- Set your alarm on your phone to go off a few times throughout the day to remind you to experience "a moment of appreciation of your pleasures." *This will change your life!*

Points to remember:

- You don't need to have a lot of stuff to have a lot of appreciation!
- Our lives are filled with multitudes of different pleasures every day. If you know what they are, you will be better at noticing them.
- There are real reasons why we don't focus on experiencing our pleasures.
- Play the happiness game.

Your Note

Secret # 7

Living a Meaningful Life:

Finding Your Greater Purpose

WHEN YOU ARE lying by the pool, sipping a cold drink on a hot summer day, knowing that all your bills have been paid, it is pretty easy to feel that life is great. Even if you are at work, dealing with everyday pressures, you can focus on your many pleasures and opportunities and you will also feel that life is great.

However, sometimes you meet people who have pretty average lives and experience all the pleasures that they do. They are generally grateful, but at the same time, there is something missing. No real fire, passion, or as I like to refer to it, spunk in their lives.

Jacob is in his senior year of university and has always been near the top of his class. By his own admission, he has lived a charmed life. He comes from a well-to-do, loving family and basically has no real worries or pressures. Interestingly enough, he is becoming less and less motivated to study and more depressed by the day.

What is the problem? Is there anything specific in his life that is lacking or particularly wrong? No. It would seem that he should be living life like it is a party, just enjoying his blessings every day, but he isn't.

The problem

Where there is a why there is a how.

—Niche

It is always the "Why?" that motivates us. Why get up in the morning? Why go to work? Why be nice to my wife and kids? Why pray to G-d?

When we are clear on the "why," we have purpose and drive. Why is life great?

The problem with Jacob and many other people is they don't know what the purpose of their life is. If you don't know what your purpose is, you won't know why it is good to be alive.

The most important question one can ask is "What am I living for?" Without clarity and direction on your life's major goals, no matter how much pleasure you have, no matter how optimistic or grateful you are, there will always be something missing.

The essence of wisdom is to know yourself

And

The essence of entertainment is the process of self discovery

And

One has to know that there are many things that you would be willing to die for. If you don't know what you are willing to die for, you have not yet begun to live!

—Rabbi Noah Weinberg.

I believe that these words of my rabbi, are the seeds to living with passion. Every one of us has a deep desire for purpose in our lives, beyond ourselves. The ability to affect humanity in a meaningful way is one of our deepest desires. Without focusing on meaningful life goals, our soul's deepest desires will be unfulfilled. People spend years trying to either find "it," or they spend their time trying to be distracted from the frustration of not connecting with "it." They don't even know what "it" is!

What is "it"? "It" is their life's purpose.

Knowing what we are living for plays a major role in our personal happiness and ability to live joyfully. It is the ultimate "why" question. The Vilna Gaon, one of the most influential rabbis in the past five hundred years, taught that it is important to recognize that "no one dies with half of their desires satisfied." If that is true, then one must ask the question: what is so special about life that it is worth the hassle of living?

If you want to experience this more:

- Understand that the key to greatness is doing a spiritual accounting.
- Every day, set aside time to ask yourself: What am I living for? What do I need to change?

Developing a Passion for Pleasure

How do you know if a person really enjoys skiing? If they are offered the chance to go to an even better ski hill than what they are used to, they jump at the opportunity. If they aren't such a skier, they don't really want the bother of going somewhere else.

The same is true with life. When we have a passion for our pleasures, we are constantly motivated to live more and get more. If the hassle of life does get us down, it is only temporary because we will be motivated in our quest for pleasures.

In Secret # 1, we spoke generally about how to clarify what you are living for; now I want to expound just a little bit more on how to develop passion in our lives.

The Passion Principle

> Even if you are passionate about something silly, you will enjoy your life more!

Passion is so powerful, that even if the most meaningful thing to you is how well your basketball team does, you will wake up in the morning with zest. You will have something to talk about, and you will be a more interesting person to be around. You invariably will find others who share your passion, and that will open you up to multitudes of other pleasures.

Of course, the real goal is to be passionate about truly meaningful, purposeful things. Things like making our communities better places to live in or developing our personal character into being less selfish and kinder people. These connect us with truth and are very satisfying pursuits. We need not only to understand how to develop passion but also to understand how to develop passion in the things that are most beneficial to us.

This concept is so important that in Jewish tradition the very first law that is stated in the law books is to; "strengthen yourself to wake up every morning like a lion, to serve your Creator." For thousands of years, Jewish consciousness has infused passion in waking up every day with enthusiasm and the purpose of getting close to G-d. The first words out of a Jewish person's mouth after awaking are "Thank you, G-d, for restoring my soul to me with mercy and giving me another day of life!" Again, the goal is to set gratitude as the first and foremost attitude of the day.

How do you develop Passion for something?

Passion Pathway # 1: Relevance

As a general rule, we only care about things that will make a difference in our lives. People have a lot going on and are very busy. Whether the topic is religion, politics, sports, or current events, as long as the topic affects us, we will be interested and therein lays the potential for passion.

If there is a topic or issue that you intuitively feel is important but just doesn't seem to light a fire in your soul, investigate its relevance in your life. Ask yourself, "What difference does this really make for me? If I'm involved more, will I become more enriched? If the 'whatever I'm talking about' goes away, will my life be negatively affected?"

It is very possible that by asking these questions, you will drop certain things that you are involved with now and will begin to invest in other areas of life.

Daryl was a wonderfully nice guy with a noncommittal attitude about everything. He was in his mid-forties, never married, and ran a business that he inherited from his father. One time, I bumped into him at a college basketball game. He had great seats, and I asked him how often he attends the games. He told me that he never misses one and that it was his life's passion. I asked him just a few simple questions like would he be okay if the NCAA closed down and he never went to another basketball game again.

It didn't take long for him to realize that whether his team won or lost it is just a form of entertainment. It really wasn't relevant or meaningful in terms of his existence.

One of the reasons that his life was so bland was because his "passion" was so irrelevant for his life. Therefore, it really wasn't a true passion after all.

On the other hand, I know of a young couple—he is a businessman and she is a doctor. They found out that their two young children had Gaucher's disease, a debilitating condition that is handicapping for life and sometimes fatal. What did they do? Together they founded an organization that was committed to finding a cure for Gaucher's disease. She conducted the medical research, and he raised the money.

There was no guarantee of success. But inasmuch as the disease affected their own children, there was no alternative but to try. The Almighty helped them, and after six years, they developed a synthetic enzyme which can effectively treat the condition. As it turned out, their two children became the first in the world to have a hopeful prognosis.

Passion Pathway # 2: Broadening your interests

Interests lead to purpose, which leads to passion, which leads to the ultimate goal of enjoyment in life.

It all starts with developing a wide range of interests. Parents who keep their children involved in just a few areas of life and don't expose them to many different things end up doing their children a great disservice. The only way to develop interest and appreciation of things is through exposure.

When I was around ten years old, my parents enrolled me in guitar lessons. My hands are very delicate and smooth, and I couldn't develop calluses on the tips of my fingers. My fingers are not very coordinated, and I have a lousy sense of rhythm. Needless to say, I didn't stick with it very long. Bring on the clarinet! My fingers did not learn how to move in sync and well, it just didn't work. I was a complete failure as a musician. At the time, I really did not enjoy any of those lessons. Today I am very grateful I went through the experience. I often listen and enjoy many different kinds of music and have a much deeper appreciation than others do. I didn't need to become a master musician to appreciate a symphony or a rock band.

Rather, because I attempted to learn how to play instruments, I look at and listen with a different ear.

My parents sent me to art camp. I found a niche playing many different kinds of sports, and they encouraged me to travel after high school. The result is that I became a person who is interested and curious about almost everything.

> **If you want to experience this more:**
>
> - Make a list of five things that you know almost nothing about. Take one hour and do a YouTube or Wikipedia search on those subjects.

Honing in on your purpose

True meaning is found when we connect with something beyond ourselves.

The Kabbalah teaches us that Adam, the first man in the Bible's Garden of Eden, was *supposed* to have lived forever. It was only after he ate from the tree that G-d told him NOT to eat from (the forbidden fruit), that the life of every human being became finite and that the state of 'death' came into being. Therefore, it is our desire for eternal life and a connection with the Infinite, that far exceeds our own limited human existence. This is implanted in our spiritual DNA.

If my world consists of only me and my concerns and my needs, I will be frustrated and in spiritual pain. This is because I am not eternal. One of the benefits of putting ourselves into situations where we are forced to take responsibility for others, like getting married or raising children, is that it pushes us to be concerned with more than just ourselves. The fact that others rely on us, forces us to expand our world. At times it is very challenging, but the conquering of self-centeredness is extremely gratifying.

What is your life's mission statement?

A mission statement is an articulation of intended purpose and objectives.

Perhaps the most powerful mission statement for one's life is recorded in the Bible:

> "Hear Israel, the Lord is G-d, the Lord is one.
> You shall love the Lord your G-d with all of your heart, all of your soul and all of your resources" (Deuteronomy 6:4-5).

The three legs of the meaningful life table

One can almost visualize the concept of one G-d as a tabletop supported by three legs. One leg is your heart, one leg is your soul and one leg is your resources.

There are three major areas in life that, if addressed properly, will propel you living a meaningful and happy life. In the same way that a table can stand solidly on three legs, so too does meaning in life require these three legs. Your *heart* refers to your spirit or what you put your emotions into. Your *soul* refers to your life or practically speaking, your time. Your *resources* refer to the use of your money.

Each concept is preceded by the action of giving. It is only by giving that we get out of ourselves. Every moment of our lives, we are either receiving from or giving to the world. At this moment, I am receiving air, heat, and kindness from others. At the same time, I'm giving creativity, sharing wisdom, and cheering others up. Giving begets giving, and receiving begets receiving. The more time I spend receiving from others, the greater my sense of entitlement grows, and the more difficult it becomes to appreciate and give to others. The more time I spend giving to others, the more I feel positive toward them and the more I become inspired to give to them.

The act of giving makes our lives meaningful. It is very positive for people who live alone to have pets because it gives them something that they are required to give to and take care of.

It has become increasingly common in prisons around the world to involve inmates into "pet therapy" programs. This is where prisoners with life sentences or on death row are given a pet, often a cat, to take care of. Having trustworthy, nonjudgmental companions has reduced the loneliness of participating inmates. Taking care of an animal is the only socially acceptable way of showing affection in prison, and the opportunity to do so has made the prisoners more receptive to psychological treatment. A study of participants found that they had higher self-esteem and self-confidence as a result of the program. In truth, everyone who puts forth a stronger effort in giving to others will also grow in their self-esteem and self-confidence.

One of the blessings that observant Jews recite after eating certain kinds of foods, involves thanking G-d for creating us with deficiencies.

It is a strange thing to thank G-d for after you have just benefited from the world!

We do this because, through our deficiencies and needs, a system is created where others have the opportunity to help and give to us. Because others also have deficiencies, we have the opportunity to give and help others. The doctor needs a car mechanic, who needs a school teacher, who needs a lawyer, who needs a cleaning person, who needs a doctor. Because of our deficiencies we are deeply connected. That gives our life meaning, purpose, and pleasure. Therefore, the way to connect properly with your purpose is to:

a. *give of your spirit,*
b. *give of your money,*
c. *give of your time.*

Giving of your Spirit

"Giving of your spirit" means sharing with others that which is most important to you.

What is it that drives you, motivates you? What do you find so important that it makes your life meaningful? Now pass it on and inspire others!

To do this properly, not only do you need to love your cause, value or passion, you also have to love the people that you want to benefit from your cause, value, or passion. If you make a great batch of cookies, you don't want to keep them all for yourself, you want others to enjoy them too!

The kabbalah teaches that the litmus test to know if someone truly loves G-d is if they wish to teach and inspire others about Him. Someone can pray all day long by themselves, but that just means that they enjoy praying. It does not mean that they have a true love of G-d. The only person in the Torah to be called "someone who loves G-d", was Abraham. This was because Abraham made it his life's mission to spread the value of having a connection with the Almighty.

If living a meaningful life requires that you share your most treasured values to the people you care about the most, then you need three things:

1) To know what your treasures are.
2) To be clear on and stay focused on whom you care about the most.

   My wife would often remind me as I would invest hundreds of hours into helping other people's children have better lives, that I also have children. The concern that maybe my own children would lose out because of my dedication to others has always helped keep me balanced.

3) To have a methodology on how to pass those treasures on.

What are some of the values you want to impart to your children?

When I was ten years old, my parents sent me away for the first time to sleep away camp in the summer. I didn't have any friends going, and I was very nervous about the whole thing. In my mother's attempt to reassure me that everything would be fine, she told me that I have nothing to worry about because everyone who meets me loves me and that I make friends very easily. I don't know if that was true before she said it. However, from that moment forward, for the rest of my life, I define myself as someone whom everybody loves. As a matter of fact, to convince me otherwise, you have to be really mean to me over a long period of time before I even begin to get the hint.

It was important to my mother that I felt loved. Eventually, she communicated that in a way and at the right time, so that I could receive the message.

In an effort to inculcate my children with certain values, every night when I put them to sleep I have them say the following prayer; "Thank you G-d for loving me so much and please help me become a great Jew!" It is important to me that my children know that G-d loves them and they should be inspired to be great Jews. I also, out of the blue, often ask my children if they are thinking about G-d. Sometimes the response is "Yes." and sometimes the response is,"Now that you asked me about it, yes.

Finding Your Spirit

There are two questions you should ask yourself that will help you "find your spirit."

1. Ask yourself, "What are the needs of the people I love, and how can I help them?"

2. Ask yourself, "What is the primary need of my generation or community?" Then pinpoint in yourself what you can do to help address the need.

Don't worry if it seems that you are part of the problem

One time, I went into a person's office for the first time. I asked him what he thinks the biggest problem facing the Jewish community in North America was. He responded, "Cute Asian girls."

He was referring to the high rate of interfaith marriages in our community today. Just then, a really cute Asian girl walked in the room; and he said, "Rabbi, meet my wife Jenny!"

This person eventually went on to promote and fund programs about developing Jewish pride.

Identify what is important to you. Learn about it. Talk about it with others. Share why it is relevant to you and why you think it is relevant for them. Involve as many people in your passion as possible. If it is worth while for you to think about and invest your life into, then it is also probably worth while for others.

If you want to experience this more:

- List two specific important concepts for your life.
- Speak about these issues with three people each day for a month.
- At the end of each week, write down what can be done to advance your cause.

Giving of your Money

Most people's relationship with money is a serious impediment for them living with the concept that *life is great*. King Solomon articulated this problem when he said, "If a person has ten, he wants a hundred, if he has a hundred, then he wants a thousand." Money is one of those things that most people will never get enough of. If they do get it, often their lives become more stressful worrying about what to do with it or how not to lose it.

How do you elevate money to help you live a meaningful life?

The biblical approach to money has always been that it is a tool. It can be used for great holiness, or it can be destructive and lead to corruption. Someone once said that money is like manure. If you put it in a big pile, all you get is a big smelly pile. If you spread it around, you make a lot of wonderful things grow.

If you want to know what a person values, look at their check stubs.

There are those who have the philosophy of just accumulating money. If you give too much money to your kids, you ruin your kids. And if you happen to get lucky with your kids, you'll ruin your grandchildren, and eventually the money's lost. Very few families keep money for generations.

People should use their money as a tool to build the world in ways that they wouldn't or couldn't normally do. Think of all the things that you would like to do to make the world a better place. For a lot of them, you probably don't have the time, education, or motivation to follow through. It might not be very fun to work in a soup kitchen or clean the floor of your house of worship, but these are examples of things that need to be done! What do you do?

Take your money and pay someone else to do these things for you.

In the same way you would pay someone to mow your lawn or fix your car, you can pay someone to be on call to help with the emotional needs of people in your community, or to teach the youth. This even works for prayer or religious scholarship. If you don't have the time, patience, or religious piety; but you know someone who does. Ancient Jewish wisdom teaches that we are never free from our responsibility to engage in making the world better, but rather we must use every resource we have to get these things done.

For the sake of being *very* clear, when it comes to religious obligations, just because you paid someone to pray or study does not absolve you *completely* from doing things yourself. You will still benefit greatly by involving your whole being in these activities in addition to using your money to bring this kind of goodness in the world.

We don't have the time or talents to do everything, but we do have some money to pay for them. The important thing is to make sure that the good things that need to get done, get done.

The Hebrew word for *charity* is *tzaduka*, which literally means "righteousness." When a person gives charity, they are bringing righteousness into the world.

How much of your money should you give?

The Bible and kabbalah teach that a person should give 10 percent of their net income to charity (This is where the expression *tithe*—one tenth—comes from). For those who wish to do more, they can give up to 20 percent. Above that amount is unrealistic. If you give too much, you'll come to neglect other aspects of your life.

In the Bible, Abraham gave 10 percent of all that he had to Melchizedek, the holy man of his generation (Genesis 14:20). Isaac anticipated his income and gave 10 percent before he even made it. G-d blessed him with one hundred times the crop that he thought he would get. Jacob also promised G-d 10 percent of his earnings and was overly blessed (Genesis 29:22). There are mandated tithes to support the Levites (Numbers 18:21, 24) and the poor (Deuteronomy 26:12).

The only area in Jewish law that wherein we are encouraged to test G-d, meaning, telling G-d "I'll do such and such and, G-d, you do this for me," is in the area of charity. The prophet tells us to test G-d by giving 20 percent of our income to charity, and G-d will financially bless us so much that our storehouses will be filled to the point where we say "Enough!"

But it is so hard to give the money!

Like most important actions in life, the giving of our money even to the most worthy of causes can be difficult. In Jewish law it actually states that it is preferable to give $10 one hundred times over than give $1,000 once. This is because we need to train our hands and hearts to give.

In most Jewish homes, one can find a *pushka* or charity box. It is a place where we on a daily basis deposit an extra dollar or extra change. When it is full, we bring it to our synagogue or whatever cause we are collecting for. It is often not a lot of money, but because it is something, everyday, it adds up. Most importantly, the action of putting money in the *pushka* reinforces the value of being righteous and giving of *tzaduka*.

The way to make giving of charity enjoyable

From a purely spiritual perspective, the Almighty gives us everything: our life, our talents, and even our money. The least we can do is to shave 10 percent off what he really owns and distribute it on his behalf. Many people set up a charity account. When they get a paycheck, or withdraw money from investments, they automatically put 10 percent of it into the charity account. This is not your money, it is G-d's money and you have the privilege of distributing it.

Psychologically, when you give of your money, even if you realize the benefit you are bringing to the world, you somehow feel less.

However, when you give of someone else's money, even if it is G-d's, you have a blast. It is only pleasurable.

The other benefit is that if you are asked to give and your charity account is empty, you won't feel as bad that you can't give now. The fact that you know you are fulfilling your charitable obligation puts your role in perspective. Eventually G-d will bless you with more money, and you will enjoy giving again.

If you want to experience this more:

- Identify two or three major recipients of your charity.
- Set up a charity account and distribute 80 percent of your funds to those causes.
- At the end of each month, evaluate if your distribution is making a difference.

Give of your Time

Our time is the only nonrenewable resource that we have. If you lose your money, you can make it back. If you get sick, you can recover. Even if you get divorced, you can find someone else and remarry. However, if you "kill an hour" or "lose a day," you can never get it back. Every one of us has an expiration date, and none of us knows when it will be.

So much of life, including how long we will live, is out of our control. What is in our control is how we use our time. Are we making the most of our days? Are we accomplishing what we need to accomplish? Are we enjoying our lives to the best of our ability?

These are the questions that ultimately lead to whether or not the hours of our days and the years of our lives were worthwhile.

Be the Best that you can Be!

There is a story about a beloved man called Reb Zusha. When he was on his deathbed surrounded by his students, he began to cry. His students tried to comfort him, saying, "Rabbi, don't be upset. You were just as kind to people than our forefather Abraham." Reb Zusha started crying even more. The students responded, "Rabbi, don't be upset. You were just as righteous as Joseph!" Reb Zusha started crying even more. His students again tried to bring comfort to him saying, "Rabbi, don't be upset. You knew as much Torah as Moses!"

As Reb Zusha regained his composure, he explained, "When I go to the next world and stand in judgment before my Creator, I am not concerned if I will be asked if I was as kind as Abraham, righteous as Josef, or as knowledgeable as Moses. What I am concerned about is when I will be asked if I was as kind as Reb Zusha could have been or as righteous as Reb Zusha could have been or did I know as much Torah as Reb Zusha could have known!"

The kabbalah compares the life we live on earth to a diamond chip that needs to be polished. Every day is represented by its own diamond chip Before a soul is put into this world, it is given a certain number of chips; when all the chips are polished, then the soul has fulfilled its mission on earth.

How do we polish the chip? When we address life's challenges and do our best to fulfill our potential in this world, we polish the chips. The biggest challenges for all of us will be associated with self-centeredness and ego.

The Talmud tells us that "anger, desire, and honor remove a person from this world." These are the three most common expressions of our selfishness and ego.

Better people make the world a better place

One of the primary ways to get out of ourselves is by giving our time to others. Dedicating our time—our very precious, valuable, limited time to making the world a better place—is the ultimate in sanctification of our lives. Whereas making the world a better place is actually a life-goal mission statement, it is so broad that for most people it could be almost meaningless. As the saying goes, "When you try to be everything to everyone, you end up being nothing to no one."

Focusing your time to help specific people or advance specific causes to benefit the world is the most effective use of your energy.

How much of your time should you give?

Just like a person should give 10 percent of their money to charity, so too should they dedicate specifically 10 percent of their time to advance their cause. If a person sleeps eight hours a day, that leaves sixteen left to tithe. That is a little more than one and a half hours a day to specifically invest in your cause that makes your life meaningful.

If you want to experience this more:

- Every night before you go to sleep, ask yourself two questions:
    - "What did I do right today?" Commit to repeating the success.
    - "What mistakes did I make today?" Commit to doing a little better tomorrow.

At the end of our lives, we all look back at our days and recount how we have made ourselves better and affected the world in a positive way. If we can recognize that we have used our time, money, and spirit in a meaningful way, we will be filled with a very deep sense of pleasure. Not only will we be filled with joy and satisfaction that our lives had purpose, but we will actualize the experience that "Life is Great!"

Points to remember:

- Identify the purpose of your life and you will be well on your way to a happier existence.
- Work on developing interests that will lead you to becoming more passionate about things that are relevant to your life.
- Become more generous with giving of your spirit, your money and your time.
- Better people make the world a better place and that makes it easier for everyone to be happier.

Your Notes

Epilogue

Putting it all together

I END IN a similar way that I began. Learning to live with the concept that "Life is Great" is not a plateau but a process. Ancient Jewish wisdom has always emphasized that life is a journey, an evolution of personal development, and that climbing the mountain is often more pleasurable than reaching the summit. Even when a person feels that they have made it, he will soon encounter another challenge.

I have presented to you a collection of pieces of wisdom from the Torah that will give you the skills necessary to live with "Life is Great." You now have what you need to ride the positive waves of life a little longer and make the valleys a little less deep and quicker to get out of.

In Judaism, the learning of Torah, Jewish wisdom, has always been considered the most important commandment and the wise man is considered the highest form of nobility. This is because of the immense power found in Torah wisdom to improve our lives. A person learns a piece of wisdom that seems to just float in his mind until a particular event occurs. Then all of a sudden, that wisdom is relevant to the situation, and it is accessed in a way that enhances the person's life.

An example of this is what happened to my friend Richard. He is an eye surgeon by profession, and in his words he had just acquired his midlife crisis car, a very expensive Mercedes Benz. He was on his way to meeting me for lunch and a little Torah study when he pulled into a parking spot. A piece of metal that was sticking up from the parking bumper cracked and broke off a small piece of his new car. Richard got out of the car to inspect the damage. He told me that in the past he would have become really upset and it would have ruined his whole day. However this time, he said to himself, "It is just a car. The really important thing is what is going to happen in the restaurant when I am studying with the rabbi." After we finished our meeting, he took the small piece of bumper that was broken off and put it in the ashtray of his car to help remind himself of something very profound. When he gets caught up in trivial things, he would look at this piece of plastic and remember; it is only a car, and there are more important things in life than whatever is annoying me at this moment.

His life is now forever transformed. Richard told me that it was because we had been meeting over the previous years that he had grown to the point of being able to keep these kinds of things in perspective.

In a similar vein, a friend of mine, Rabbi Irwin Katzof in his book, *How to Get Your Prayers Answered* tells the following story of a woman by the name of Uriela.

Uriela decided to take a trip into the Sinai Peninsula, hoping for a spiritual experience. This was the place where the Israelites had their profound encounter with G-d, which changed them and the world forever. Uriela was hoping that some of those spiritual vibrations would still be hanging around.

However, before she embarked on her trip, she found herself in a class learning a piece of Torah, which discussed one of Abraham's encounters with G-d. It was the third day after Abraham had circumcised himself, he was in a lot of pain, and G-d was visiting Abraham. Abraham could see in the distance three travelers. He interrupted his visit with the Almighty to run after the travelers and extend an invitation to bring them to his tent for dinner.

In an attempt to explain Abraham's behavior, the rabbi who was teaching the class asked the question, "Is there anything more important in life than speaking with G-d?" "Yes," the rabbi answered, "being like G-d!" He continued to explain that emulating the Almighty's ways in performing acts of kindness, being merciful, and exhibiting patience were aspects of the highest forms of holiness and connection with G-d.

Uriela then started her trip. The goal was to see the sunset from the highest spot in the Sinai open to the public, Mount Abbas Basha. It took three hours by Bedouin cab, three hours by camel, and another two hours walking. She found herself in stunning territory, surrounded by mammoth, wind-shorn rocks reaching into the sky. Completely devoid of anything to distract her from her G-dly experience, she was feeling the awesomeness of the moment.

Just then, the stillness of the air was broken by the chattering of three hikers. She was very surprised to see anyone and became annoyed when the hikers decided to rest next to her little encampment. "Can't they find another place to sit?" she muttered to her guide. "They've got the whole Sinai, why do they choose to impinge on my space?"

Then it hit her. It wasn't her space; it was G-d's space. And how different was her attitude toward these three strangers than Abraham's had been toward his three travelers. She did an immediate 180-degree spin and offered the hikers some of her food.

"No, thank you," they said, and promptly left.

Uriela is convinced today that they were sent there for a very specific purpose. She had prayed for a spiritual experience and her prayers were answered, although not in the way she had imagined.

This trip to the Sinai proved to be a redefining experience for Uriela, and because of it, she changed her whole life to engage in acts of hospitality and kindness. She started a process of self-examination. Her whole life she thought of herself as a good person; in actuality, she just was not a bad person. Going out of her way to do acts of kindness and bring pleasure to others was not part of her life plan, until now.

The important factor is that she never would have gotten the message if she had not learned the story of Abraham before the trip. The strangers would have come, sat down, annoyed her, and she would have no idea what to make of it. It would have been like a radio broadcast sent out without any receiver to bring it in.

This is why the Kabbala teaches that in order to hear G-d's messages, a person must study the Torah and other aspects of Jewish wisdom.

The true value in all the concepts that have been written in this book will not be found in a one-time reading. Akin to perfecting a free throw shot in basketball, the key is practice, practice, and practice. If you truly wish to live "Life is Great," I suggest that you continuously review the main principles until they become second nature to you. Like Richard and Uriela, they will swim in your head unnoticed until the precise moment when they will appear and help make your life great.

I have prepared the following ten-day program of review. On the left is a number. On the day of the month that ends with that number, you should read, think about, and explore the concept on the right. For example, the number 1, you should review that concept on the first, eleventh, twenty-first, and thirty-first of each month. The number 2, you will review the concept on the second, twelfth, and twenty-second of the month. For the number 0, you will review that concept on the tenth, twentieth, and thirteenth day of each month,and so on. This way you will go through each concept at least three times every month.

At the beginning, I would encourage you to go through the chapter in the book that discusses the concept. Eventually, I think you will find it valuable to explore other resources that will help you appreciate the depths of these principles. Rabbi Zelig Pliskin's *Gateway to Happiness*, Dennis Prager's *Happiness Is a Serious Problem* and *Happy for No Reason* by Marci Shimoff are among my favorites.

10 steps of review for 10 days

1 ~ Happiness is the pleasure one feels when they appreciate that life is good, and it is created when we focus on what we have.
- Take a few moments today and focus on how wonderful it is to be alive.

2 ~ Ask yourself the most important question—what am I living for?
- Articulate several times over the answer.
- Now reflect on how your actions illustrate your values to the world around you.

3 ~ The ultimate secret to happiness—taking pleasure in what you have. Make a list of your blessings.
- Express your gratitude to the person or entity that gave you the blessings.

4 ~ Happiness is More than just a choice, it is an obligation to yourself, to others and to G-d.
- Spend the day intentionally acting happier than you normally would.

5 ~ Create a positive visualization of living the way you want to be.
- Perform specific actions that reflect your visions.

6 ~ According to the effort is the reward—this applies to everything, even happiness.
- Enjoy putting for the effort to intentionally be more grateful and optimistic.

7 ~ The most important concept a parent can impress upon their children is to know that Life is Great!

- Set an example for others today as a person who knows it is great to be alive.

8 ~ Give of your spirit, your time, and your money to make the world a better place.

- Increase your level of passion for things by dedicating a little more of your time, energy, and money to your cause today.

9 ~ Create things and events to look forward to.

- Make specific plans with people you care about.

0 ~ Notice your five levels of pleasures: physical, love, doing the right thing, being creative, and connecting all pleasures to G-d.

- Take a few moments several times today to identify the specific pleasures that you are experiencing.

My hope and prayer is that this short book has intellectually and spiritually enriched you. In helping you live that "Life is Great," together we will make the world a better place.

—Rabbi Yitz Wyne

CPSIA information can be obtained at www.ICGtesting.com
Printed in the USA
LVOW06s2341240414

383191LV00004B/104/P

9 781456 869434